S. Hrg. 114–330

THE BUREAU OF LAND MANAGEMENT'S FINAL RULE ON HYDRAULIC FRACTURING

HEARING

BEFORE THE

SUBCOMMITTEE ON PUBLIC LANDS, FORESTS, AND MINING

OF THE

COMMITTEE ON ENERGY AND NATURAL RESOURCES UNITED STATES SENATE

ONE HUNDRED FOURTEENTH CONGRESS

FIRST SESSION

APRIL 30, 2015

Printed for the use of the
Committee on Energy and Natural Resources

Available via the World Wide Web: http://www.fdsys.gov

U.S. GOVERNMENT PUBLISHING OFFICE

95–274   WASHINGTON : 2016

For sale by the Superintendent of Documents, U.S. Government Publishing Office
Internet: bookstore.gpo.gov Phone: toll free (866) 512–1800; DC area (202) 512–1800
Fax: (202) 512–2104 Mail: Stop IDCC, Washington, DC 20402–0001

CONTENTS

OPENING STATEMENTS

WITNESSES

ALPHABETICAL LISTING AND APPENDIX MATERIAL SUBMITTED

THE BUREAU OF LAND MANAGEMENT'S FINAL RULE ON HYDRAULIC FRACTURING

THURSDAY, APRIL 30, 2015

U.S. SENATE
SUBCOMMITTEE ON PUBLIC LANDS, FORESTS, AND MINING
COMMITTEE ON ENERGY AND NATURAL RESOURCES
Washington, DC.

The Subcommittee met, pursuant to notice, at 2:31 p.m. in Room SD–366, Dirksen Senate Office Building, Hon. John Barrasso, Chairman of the Subcommittee, presiding.

OPENING STATEMENT OF HON. JOHN BARRASSO, U.S. SENATOR FROM WYOMING

Senator BARRASSO. The committee will come to order.

This afternoon the Subcommittee on Public Lands, Forests, and Mining will hold its first hearing of the 114th Congress. I am pleased to chair this subcommittee, and I look forward to working with the Subcommittee's Ranking Member, Senator Wyden. He and I visited a little earlier. He has a packed schedule and will try to make it to the subcommittee hearing. Other members have conflicts but will also try to be here to hear the testimony and take part in the questioning.

Senator Wyden has always been an engaging and willing listener when he chaired this panel, and I intend to extend the same courtesy to him and to all members of the committee.

The Public Lands Subcommittee is especially important to my home State of Wyoming. In Wyoming, about 47 percent of the surface estate and 67 percent of the mineral estate is owned by the Federal Government. This means that decisions made in Washington have an extraordinary impact on the people of Wyoming.

As Chairman, I will ensure that we bring scrutiny to these decisions, especially those that put Federal lands in the West at a competitive disadvantage to other areas of the country when it comes to energy and specifically mineral production.

Today, this subcommittee will examine the Bureau of Land Management's final rule on hydraulic fracturing. BLM issued its final rule on March 20th, 2015. It is scheduled to take effect on June 24th. I continue to believe that the BLM's rule is a solution in search of a problem. Wyoming has among the strictest hydraulic fracturing regulations in the country, and these regulations already apply to Federal lands within our state.

In 2013, the Wyoming delegation called on Secretary Jewell to exempt Wyoming and other states from this rule.

[The information referred to follows:]

Congress of the United States
Washington, DC 20510

August 19, 2013

The Honorable Sally Jewell
Secretary of the Interior
U.S. Department of the Interior
1849 C Street, NW, Room 5665
Washington, D.C. 20240

Dear Secretary Jewell:

We are writing today to express our concern about the Bureau of Land Management's (BLM) proposed rule on hydraulic fracturing published in the *Federal Register* on May 24, 2013. BLM's proposed rule duplicates, in many aspects, state regulations that already address well-bore integrity and flowback water and require the disclosure of hydraulic fracturing constituents used on Federal public lands. We believe that BLM's proposed rule will significantly delay oil and gas permitting and in turn discourage oil and gas production on our nation's public lands.

In contrast to most states, public land states face a number of challenges relating to the management of land and minerals within their borders. For example, those looking to gain access to our nation's public lands must comply not only with state law, but also with Federal law. Federal law and regulations often delay investment and job creation for years. Consequently, Federal law and regulations push investment out of public land states and into other states where there is greater regulatory certainty. On March 14, 2012, then BLM Director, Bob Abbey, testified that there has been "a shift [in oil and gas production] to private lands in the East and to the South where there are fewer amounts of Federal mineral estate." We believe BLM's final rule will contribute to this shift in oil and gas production and cost public land states, Indian tribes, and the Federal government hundreds of millions of dollars in revenue.

We also question whether BLM's final rule will provide any meaningful benefits not already provided by public land states. Public land states, such as Wyoming, Colorado, Idaho, Montana, New Mexico, and Utah, currently enforce their own hydraulic fracturing regulations, including regulations requiring the disclosure of hydraulic fracturing constituents. These state regulations not only apply to private and state lands, but also apply or could be applied to Federal public lands within the states' respective borders. On June 6, 2013, you were asked before the Senate Energy and Natural Resources Committee which states currently regulating hydraulic fracturing are not doing a sufficient job. Your inability to identify any state suggests, at the very least, that BLM's final rule should not apply to states currently regulating hydraulic fracturing.

In conclusion, we believe that states are best positioned to regulate hydraulic fracturing. We appreciate your acknowledgment that Wyoming has "great, sophisticated" hydraulic fracturing regulations and is "a good example of a state that is doing an effective job." We therefore request that you exempt Wyoming and the other states currently regulating hydraulic fracturing from

BLM's final rule. State regulations are a solution that is working for the people of our nation's public land states. They should be supported, not supplanted, by the Administration.

Sincerely,

Michael B. Enzi
U.S. Senator

John Barrasso, M.D.
U.S. Senator

Cynthia M. Lummis
U.S. Representative

Secretary Jewell rejected this request and instead provided states with an opportunity to obtain a so-called variance from the BLM's rule. I am interested to know how the variance process works and whether states have any interest in pursuing it.

I am also interested in understanding the larger impact that this rule and other regulations will have on oil and gas production in the West. In addition to the hydraulic fracturing rule, the Obama Administration plans to issue three other major rules for oil and gas on Federal lands. The Administration plans to issue a new rule for natural gas venting and flaring and also rules which would increase royalty rates. These regulations and those the Administration has already imposed have put Wyoming and the West at an even greater disadvantage to other areas of the country.

According to the Energy Information Administration (EIA), Federal onshore natural gas production has decreased by 22 percent since 2009. EIA has found that Federal onshore natural gas production makes up a smaller percentage of total U.S. gas production than it has in the last 11 years. Federal onshore oil production also makes up a smaller percentage of total U.S. oil production than it has in nine years. While these numbers reflect new production on State and private lands, they also show that Federal lands are becoming less competitive with State and private lands.

Oil and gas production provides thousands of good-paying jobs in the West. These jobs are available to individuals from all walks of life. They are jobs that can support an entire family and allow parents to send their kids to college. The people of Wyoming want these jobs, and I will fight to keep them in our state.

If BLM wants to be a good neighbor to the people of Wyoming and other Western states, I think it must not only listen to their concerns but be responsive to them. Mr. Kornze, I expect you to lead in that effort.

Senator Wyden will offer opening remarks if he arrives.

Senator BARRASSO. At this point I would like to welcome our witnesses. Joining us this afternoon is the Honorable Neil Kornze, Director of the Bureau of Land Management; Mr. Bruce Baizel, the Energy Program Director of Earthworks; Ms. Kathleen Sgamma, Vice President of the Western Energy Alliance; and Mr. Mark Watson, the Supervisor of the Wyoming Oil and Gas Conservation Commission. Welcome to all of you. I look forward to the testimony, and your complete statements will be included in the record. If you could keep your testimony to five minutes, I would certainly appreciate it. Mr. Kornze, we will begin with you.

STATEMENT OF HON. NEIL KORNZE, DIRECTOR, BUREAU OF LAND MANAGEMENT, U.S. DEPARTMENT OF THE INTERIOR

Mr. KORNZE. Thank you, Mr. Chairman. It is great to be here with you today. I appreciate the invitation.

The Bureau of Land Management manages nearly 250,000,000 acres of surface property and 700,000,000 acres of subsurface estate in the nation. That equates to 10 percent of the nation's surface and nearly a third of its minerals and soils. We manage these lands under the dual mission of multiple use and sustained yield.

The Bureau's work is now more complex than ever, and the professionals at the BLM have to make very difficult choices every day, but throughout that work we make sure that the public has a very strong voice in the work that we do.

More than 450,000 jobs were supported by the agency and the lands that we managed last year, and we are one of only a handful of agencies that returns more dollars than we receive in appropriations. In fact, for every dollar you appropriate here in Congress, we return $5.

The BLM works diligently to fulfill its role in securing America's energy future by supporting the development of oil and gas resources on public and Indian lands. From 2008 to last year, oil production from those lands increased 81 percent. Now, that increase has tracked or exceeded trends on comparable State and private lands. Now, natural gas has gone down in recent years, but this too has generally tracked the rate of production on nearby private and State lands.

Overall in Fiscal Year 2014, onshore Federal oil and gas royalties exceeded $3 billion and tribal royalties exceeded $1 billion. The BLM is proud to play a critical role in meeting the nation's energy needs, and with even more than 100,000 wells to monitor and oversee, we continue to make lands for oil and gas development available in excess of industry demand. Right now, the industry has roughly 34,000,000 acres under lease, but it is only producing from a third of those lands. And last year, the BLM approved 4,400 drilling permits and nearly a third of those permits went unused. In total, the industry now holds roughly 6,000 permits that are available for use today with no further review, no further permitting. They are ready to go. That equates to roughly two years worth of drilling potential on public lands. We would like to see those permits used to bring American jobs and American energy forward.

In supporting this energy development, our oil and gas program's highest priority is ensuring that operations are safe and responsible. The hydraulic fracturing rule is critical to meeting that responsibility.

Over 90 percent of the wells that are drilled on public lands are hydraulically fractured using techniques that are significantly more complex than those of the past. Today's wells are often much deeper and coupled with advanced horizontal drilling techniques, which are quite incredible.

While these technological advances and the tremendous increase in their use has facilitated greater access to oil and gas resources, it has also necessitated that the BLM revisit its existing rules, which were last updated over 30 years ago. The BLM's new rule establishes reasonable, common sense standards requiring operators to construct sound wells, to disclose the chemicals they use, and to safely recover the wastewater that comes back from that drilling process. This rule establishes a baseline that many operators are comfortable with because they are in many places already implementing the practices that we have required.

Our rule was informed by the technical expertise of our engineers in the field, as well as that of state regulators, Indian regulators, and industry. The final rule specifically recognizes the experience and expertise of our partners.

We have a track record at the BLM of working successfully with states and others to make sure that we avoid duplication and delay, and the implementation of the hydraulic fracturing rule will be no different. We are actively working with many states and tribes that have standards in place for hydraulic fracturing to evaluate potential variances from various aspects of the BLM rule. These discussions will continue as we work closely with states and tribes to ensure successful implementation.

Mr. Chairman, members of the committee, the BLM's rule establishes common sense standards that are essential to protecting our shared environment while also making sure that we have robust energy development in this nation.

I appreciate the time.

[The prepared statement of Mr. Kornze follows:]

Statement of
Neil Kornze
Director
Bureau of Land Management, U.S. Department of the Interior
Senate Energy and Natural Resources Committee
Subcommittee on Public Lands, Forests, and Mining

"Bureau of Land Management's Final Hydraulic Fracturing Rule"

April 30, 2015

Chairman Barrasso, Ranking Member Wyden, and Members of the Subcommittee, thank you for the opportunity to discuss the Bureau of Land Management's (BLM) final hydraulic fracturing regulations and their application to Federal, tribal, and Indian trust mineral resources. The BLM oil and gas program's highest priority is ensuring that the operations it authorizes on public and tribal lands are safe and environmentally responsible. This rule is critical to meeting that responsibility as we continue to offer millions of acres of public land for minerals development each year.

The BLM's rule establishes a consistent set of requirements designed to prevent problems in these complex hydraulic fracturing operations before they occur. It also will provide as much information as possible to the public about these operations that affect their public lands. The goals of the rule – safe and environmentally responsible operation and resource protection – are goals that we know the BLM shares with industry, states, tribes, and the American public. The expertise brought to these issues by those who participated in the rulemaking process was essential to producing a rule that will achieve these goals, and we are very appreciative of the time and skill invested by all concerned.

Background
The BLM is responsible for protecting the resources and managing the uses of our nation's public lands, which are located primarily in 12 western states, including Alaska. The BLM administers more land – over 245 million surface acres – than any other Federal agency. The BLM also manages approximately 700 million acres of onshore Federal mineral estate throughout the nation, including the subsurface estate overlain by properties managed by other Federal agencies such as the Department of Defense and the U.S. Forest Service. In addition, the BLM, together with the Bureau of Indian Affairs (BIA), provides permitting and oversight services under the Indian Mineral Leasing Act of 1938 to approximately 56 million acres of land held in trust by the Federal government on behalf of tribes and individual Indian owners. The BLM works closely with surface management agencies, including the BIA and tribal governments, in the management of these subsurface resources. We are also mindful of our agency's responsibility for stewardship of public land resources and Indian trust assets that generate substantial revenue for the U.S. Treasury, the states, tribal governments, and individual Indian owners.

In support of President Obama's all-of-the-above energy strategy, the BLM is committed to promoting safe, responsible, and environmentally sustainable domestic oil and gas production in a manner that will protect consumers, human health, and the environment, and reduce our dependence on foreign oil. Secretary Jewell has made it clear that as we expand and diversify our energy portfolio, the development of conventional energy resources from BLM-managed lands will continue to play a critical role in meeting the nation's energy needs and fueling our economy.

In Fiscal Year (FY) 2014, onshore Federal oil and gas royalties exceeded $3 billion, approximately half of which were paid directly to the states in which the development occurred. In FY 2014, tribal oil and gas royalties exceeded $1 billion with all of those revenues paid to the tribes or individual Indian owners of the land on which the development occurred.

The BLM works diligently to fulfill its role in securing America's energy future, coordinating closely with partners across the country to ensure that development of oil and gas resources occurs in the right places and that those projects are managed safely and responsibly. In recent years, the BLM has overseen a significant increase in oil production from public lands, while also supporting continued natural gas production. Oil production from Federal and Indian lands in 2014 rose twelve percent from the previous year and is now up 81 percent since 2008 – 113 million barrels per year in 2008 to 205 million barrels per year today. For comparison, nationwide oil production over the same period increased 73 percent. The BLM is proud to be a leader in this area, and continues to make public lands available for oil and gas development in excess of industry demand. Additionally, today the BLM has responsibility for more than 100,000 existing oil and gas wells.

Hydraulic Fracturing Technology
Hydraulic fracturing involves the injection of fluid under high pressure to create or enlarge fractures in the rocks containing oil and gas so that the fluids can flow more freely into the wellbore and thus increase production. The number of wells on BLM-managed public lands and on Indian lands that are stimulated by hydraulic fracturing techniques has increased steadily in recent years. Of wells currently being drilled, over 90 percent use modern hydraulic fracturing techniques for well completion.

These new well completions are typically significantly more complex than the wells drilled in the past. Modern hydraulic fracturing operations are often considerably deeper and coupled with relatively new horizontal drilling techniques, unlike those that occurred in the past which were used on a relatively small scale to complete or to re-complete wells. The increasingly common combination of long lateral well bores with hydraulic fracturing today has facilitated larger-scale operations that allow greater access to shale oil and gas resources across the country, sometimes in areas that have not previously or only recently experienced significant oil and gas development.

Hydraulic Fracturing Rulemaking Considerations
The Mineral Leasing Act of 1920 (MLA), as amended, directs the Secretary of the Interior to lease Federal oil and gas resources, and authorizes her to regulate the resulting oil and gas operations on those leases. The BLM has used this authority to develop regulations governing all aspects of oil and gas operations, including requirements related to surface-disturbing activities, production measurement, and well construction. The Indian Mineral Leasing Act

extends this regulatory authority and the resultant rules to Indian oil and gas leases on trust lands (except those lands specifically excluded by statute). Finally, the Federal Land Policy and Management Act of 1976 (FLPMA) directs the BLM to manage the public lands using the principles of multiple use and sustained yield and to take any action necessary to prevent unnecessary or undue degradation. In fulfilling these objectives, FLPMA requires the BLM to manage public lands in a manner that protects the quality of their resources, including ecological, environmental, and water resources. On net, this statutory regime requires the BLM to balance responsible development with protection of the environment and public safety. The BLM works hard to ensure the appropriate balance is struck and that the applicable regulations and requirements are applied and enforced fairly and consistently across all the lands where the BLM has oversight responsibilities.

Prior to the issuance of the hydraulic fracturing rule, the BLM's rules on oil and gas operations were last updated over 30 years ago, and had not kept pace with the significant technological advances in hydraulic fracturing techniques and the tremendous increase in its use. The new rule is the culmination of four years of work by the BLM that began in November 2010 when it held its first public forum on this topic. Since that time, the BLM has published two proposed rules and held numerous meetings with the public and state officials, as well as many tribal consultations and meetings. The public comment period was open for a cumulative period of more than 210 days, during which time the BLM received and analyzed comments from more than 1.5 million individuals and groups. During this period, the BLM also studied state and tribal regulations, and consulted with state and tribal agencies, industry, and the public, including communities affected by oil and gas operations.

Hydraulic Fracturing Rule Requirements

Informed by the experience of its experts and the technical expertise and concerns of state regulators, tribes, industry, and the public, the BLM's hydraulic fracturing rule strengthens its existing oversight procedures and provides all stakeholders with additional assurance that operations are being carried out safely and responsibly.

Key components of the rule include provisions for ensuring the protection of groundwater supplies through requirements related to wellbore integrity. These include the placement of strong cement barriers between the wellbore and any potentially usable water zones through which the wellbore passes, which protects groundwater both from hydraulic fracturing fluids during drilling and from hydrocarbon contamination during production. The rule requires the interim storage of recovered waste fluids from the hydraulic fracturing operation in tanks in order to minimize the potential for produced water spills that put air, water, and wildlife at risk. Additional measures requiring companies to submit more detailed information on the geology, depth, and location of preexisting wells prior to drilling will lower the risk of cross-well contamination, which has become more prevalent as the prevalence of horizontal drilling has increased. To increase transparency, as much of this information as possible will be made available to the public. Finally, the rule requires companies to publicly disclose information about the chemicals used in their hydraulic fracturing processes on public lands within 30 days of completing the operations.

These requirements were developed based on BLM's experience and technical expertise and work done by states, tribal authorities, and industry. During the four years the BLM spent preparing the rule, it benefited from the expertise of state and tribal regulators, and many provisions of the final rule reflect existing state standards. None of these requirements impose undue delays, costs, or procedures on operators.

Work with States & Tribes

The BLM has established and maintained regulations governing oil and gas operations on public lands for decades, and has worked successfully with operators, tribes and state governments to avoid duplication and delay in the enforcement and monitoring of these regulations. The implementation of the recently issued hydraulic fracturing rule will continue this longstanding practice while also ensuring the BLM satisfies its obligations to ensure federal standards are met. As explained above, the rule builds upon and updates the BLM's existing regulations to address an evolving technology, in order to provide consistent parameters for the conduct of hydraulic fracturing operations on BLM-managed public lands nationwide and Indian trust lands.

Of the 32 states with the potential for oil and gas development on federally managed mineral resources, slightly more than half have rules in place that address hydraulic fracturing, and those rules vary widely from state to state. Recognizing the expertise and experience that state and tribal authorities possess and consistent with its standard practice of ensuring the efficient implementation of its rules, the BLM will work with states and tribes that have standards in place for hydraulic fracturing that meet or exceed those set by the BLM's rule to establish variances from those aspects of the BLM rule. Following BLM approval of a variance, the BLM and the state or tribe will enforce the more protective requirement. In addition, the BLM will continue its coordination with states and tribes to establish or review and strengthen existing agreements related to oil and gas regulation and operations.

The BLM's overall intent for these coordination efforts is to minimize duplication and maximize efficiency, while also ensuring the applicable federal standards are met. As this rule is implemented, the BLM will continuously work with states, tribes, and operators to maximize coordination and efficiency.

Implementing the Rule

The final hydraulic fracturing rule will be effective on June 24, 2015. Implementation of the rule is expected to cost industry about $11,400 per hydraulic fracturing operation. On average, this expense equates to no more than one-quarter of one percent of the cost of drilling a well. This is a modest cost, especially in light of public interest in ensuring that these operations are conducted in an environmentally sound and safe manner. The BLM is aware that industry, states, tribes, and the public share the same goal of safeguarding local communities, water quality, wildlife, and other resources from potential harm. For this reason, the BLM rule not only incorporates requirements from existing state and tribal rules, but industry best practices as well. In many cases operators have voluntarily undertaken the best practices reflected in the BLM's rule. The rule ensures that those practices are maintained and adopted by all. As result, the rule achieves a cost-effective path towards consistent permitting requirements and disclosure protocols for hydraulic fracturing operations.

The BLM has taken a number of steps both internally and externally to prepare for the implementation of the rule in advance of its effective date. Internally, recognizing the central role wellbore integrity plays in maintaining safe operations, the BLM partnered with the Society of Petroleum Engineers to add more technical training for the BLM's engineers that emphasizes cementing and other critical aspects of hydraulic fracturing operations. As the BLM implements the rule, it will continue to offer, develop and refine these technical training modules. Guidance will also be issued to State and Field Offices through formal Instruction Memorandum to ensure the rule is implemented in the most efficient and consistent way possible.

Externally, the BLM has undertaken outreach efforts to states, operators, trade associations, and other interested stakeholders. The BLM State Offices are in the process of meeting with their state counterparts, undertaking state-by-state comparisons of regulatory requirements in order to identify opportunities for variances, and to establish Memorandums of Understanding (MOUs) that will realize efficiencies and allow for successful implementation of the rule. To date, the BLM has scheduled or is scheduling meetings with: the North Dakota Industrial Commission; the Wyoming Oil and Gas Commission; and the states of Alaska, California, Colorado, New Mexico, Nevada, and Utah. The BLM will be presenting the rule at the Interstate Oil and Gas Compact Commission's next meeting.

Similarly, communication with industry is also ongoing. Our offices are reaching out to local or regional industry organizations and local operators to address their questions related to the implementation process. On April 7, 2015, BLM Washington hosted a general industry outreach session that over 200 people participated in to explain the rule and answer questions about its implementation. Similar sessions have been set up or will be set up at the local level. The BLM's Carlsbad NM Field Office provided a presentation to the local working group for the SE NM New Mexico Oil and Gas Association on April 9, 2015. BLM State and Field Offices are working to coordinate similar opportunities with associations representing producers in Wyoming, Utah, Colorado, Montana, and North Dakota. Finally, we are also working closely with the Ground Water Protection Council (GWPC) to finalize a MOU that will ensure that the chemical disclosures provided by industry can be easily searched and downloaded from the GWPC's publicly available hydraulic fracturing database, FracFocus.

Conclusion
The BLM's hydraulic fracturing rule provides a much needed update to the BLM's existing regulations. It establishes commonsense standards governing modern hydraulic fracturing operations that reflect the technological advancement of the process over time. These new regulations are essential to our efforts to protect the environment and local communities, while also ensuring the continued conscientious development of our federal oil and gas resources. Thank you for the opportunity to present this testimony. I will be pleased to answer any questions you may have.

Senator BARRASSO. Thank you, Mr. Kornze.
Mr. Baizel?

STATEMENT OF BRUCE BAIZEL, ENERGY PROGRAM DIRECTOR, EARTHWORKS

Mr. BAIZEL. Chairman Barrasso, Ranking Member, other members of the subcommittee, thank you very much for the opportunity to testify before you on the Bureau of Land Management's hydraulic fracturing rule. My name is Bruce Baizel. I am the Energy Program Director at Earthworks.

It is Earthworks' hope and the hope of the many communities we work with on the ground who experience the impacts of oil and gas development that we transition using our public lands for clean, renewable energy, not polluting fossil fuels, in addition to the recreational opportunities we all enjoy. My wife is a ski instructor. She works on public lands. We certainly enjoy that.

Until that transition, we feel it is important to take steps to carefully regulate the oil and gas industry to minimize harm to our natural resources and public lands. Over roughly the last 15 years, the shale revolution has spread across our country. The BLM, however, has not updated its oil and gas regulations since the 1980's. In the absence of updated rules to accommodate this rapidly growing industry, states have created a patchwork of regulations that continue to evolve with changing industry practices. Yet, a new poll from the University of Texas was released today that makes it clear that there is support for these new regulations. 60 percent of Americans support stronger oversight of hydraulic fracturing on public lands.

While there are many more regulatory improvements that could be made, the BLM's final rule governing hydraulic fracturing creates a minimum standard, a basic level of protection for our public lands, the water that flows through them, and the citizens that enjoy their use daily. It also delivers the regulatory certainty and consistency that the oil and gas industry said it desires.

The facts are clear. Many states and operators already follow the directives contained in the rule, and for these, the compliance costs will be negligible. The average well costs about $5 million to drill, yet this rule adds only a few thousand dollars to that cost. For operators who already follow these reasonable standards, the rule will provide little change from business as usual.

This rule also provides states with flexibility by providing a waiver procedure for states whose rules are at least as protective as the BLM rule. This will ensure that these rules are not duplicative of what states currently have in place while also allowing states to pass more stringent regulations if they so desire.

I sit on the board of an organization called STRONGER, which stands for the State Review of Oil and Natural Gas Environmental Regulations. That organization works toward the continuous improvement of state oil and gas regulations. We are a nonprofit, multi-stakeholder organization that includes representatives from state government, industry, and environmental representatives. I am one of three environmental representatives.

I was part of STRONGER's original workgroup that in 2009 and 2010 developed the hydraulic fracturing guideline that states should follow. So far, only six states have had STRONGER review their hydraulic fracturing regulations, and only one of these states has significant public lands, Colorado. Montana and Utah have never been reviewed. Wyoming was last reviewed in 1994, New Mexico in 2001, and California in 2002, years before the current shale oil and gas boom.

The result is that neither the public nor policymakers have a real sense of whether states have the necessary regulations in place to effectively protect the people and the environment from the impacts of oil and gas development.

Studies performed by Resources for the Future and the Groundwater Protection Council illustrate the variations and inconsistencies on everything from casing standards to definitions of usable groundwater among the Western states with significant public minerals. Some states have lessened the risks of groundwater contamination from hydraulic fracturing, my own state being an example, by tightening their regulations in the areas of well integrity, casing, cementing, chemical disclosure, and waste disposal, but others have not.

BLM commonly enters into a memorandum of understanding with states to help achieve better coordination. Colorado's memorandum of understanding was signed in 2009.

The variance procedure within the BLM hydraulic fracturing rule also fosters this type of cooperation. Rather than duplicating, the rule supplements in areas where states have yet to make important upgrades. Without the baseline standard provided in this rule, BLM would be putting all taxpayers at risk as the owners of public land and public minerals.

Thank you for the opportunity to present the views of Earthworks on this important topic, and we appreciate the committee's consideration of this important issue.

[The prepared statement of Mr. Baizel follows:]

Bruce Baizel
Energy Program Director
Earthworks

EARTHWORKS

April 30, 2015

Senate Energy and Natural Resources Subcommittee on Public Lands, Forests, and Mining

Testimony of Bruce Baizel, Energy Program Director, Earthworks

Chairman Barrasso, Ranking Member Wyden and Members of the Subcommittee:

Thank you for the opportunity to testify before you on the Bureau of Land Managements
hydraulic fracturing rule. My name is Bruce Baizel, Director of Energy Programs at Earthworks,
a national nonprofit organization that protects communities and the environment from harmful
energy development while seeking sustainable solutions.

Over approximately the last fifteen years, the so-called Shale Revolution has spread across our
country. The Bureau of Land Management (BLM), however, has not updated its oil and gas
regulations since the 1980s. In the absence of updated rules to accommodate this rapidly growing
industry, states have created a patchwork of regulations that continue to evolve with changing
industry practices.

This BLM rule creates a minimum standard, a basic level of protection for our public lands, the
water that flows through them and the citizens that enjoy their use daily. It also delivers the
regulatory certainty and consistency the oil and gas industry has said it desires. Under this rule,
states will continue to develop and adapt their hydraulic fracturing regulations as technology
improves or problems develop. This rule allows for that flexibility by providing a waiver
procedure for states whose rules are at least as protective as the BLM rule. This will ensure that
these rules are not duplicative of what states currently have in place, while also allowing states to
pass more stringent regulations if they so desire.

**I. It is doubtful whether state regulation of hydraulic fracturing has kept up with changes
in shale development**

It is difficult to say with certainty whether state regulation of hydraulic fracturing has kept pace
with shale development. I sit on the board of an organization called STRONGER (the State
Review of Oil and Natural Gas Environmental Regulations) that works toward the continuous
improvement of state regulations. STRONGER is a non-profit multi-stakeholder organization
that includes representatives from state governments, industry, and environmental
representatives. I was part of STRONGER's original workgroup that in 2009 and 2010

Bruce Baizel
Energy Program Director
Earthworks

developed the hydraulic fracturing guideline states should follow. So far, only six states have had a STRONGER review of their hydraulic fracturing regulations.

Since the onset of the shale gas boom, of the Western states with significant BLM mineral development, only Colorado has undergone any kind of STRONGER review of either its general oil and gas, or hydraulic fracturing specific, regulations. Montana and Utah have never been reviewed. Wyoming was last reviewed in 1994, New Mexico in 2001, and California in 2002 – years before the shale oil and gas boom.

The result is that, as long as states do not step up to have STRONGER review their regulations, neither the public nor policy makers have an independent sense of whether states have the necessary regulations in place to effectively protect the people and the environment from the impacts of oil and gas development.

Even if states had those protections, regulations mean nothing without adequate enforcement. We were recently asked to evaluate six states from an enforcement perspective, looking at staffing, inspection numbers, violations, sanctions and penalties and tracking of, and response to, citizen complaints. We looked at Colorado, New Mexico, Texas, Ohio, New York and Pennsylvania. Some of our findings included:

• In all states, the number of wells that do not get inspected is immense. For example, in 2010 Pennsylvania inspectors were unable to monitor approximately 81,000 active wells (89% of the state's active wells), Ohio failed to inspect more than 58,000 wells (91% of active wells), and Texas inspectors did not make it to approximately 161,000 wells (57% of active wells).

• Enforcement actions do not appear to be consistently applied in most states. New Mexico was particularly notable in the discretion afforded to inspectors to decide whether or not to issue a Letter of Violation. As a result, operators may receive different treatment simply because their site was visited by inspector X instead of inspector Y.

• In most states, we did not find that increased inspection levels resulted in less contamination. For example, in Colorado, in fiscal year (FY) 2011, 133 of the 513 reported spills (or 26%) contaminated either ground or surface water.

II. BLM is simply doing what any responsible regulator would do – adapting its regulations to changing industry practice.

National public lands need national standards that are not subject to the vagaries of state politics, budgets and varying levels of expertise. BLM's rule sets that standard while providing certainty and consistency for operators. As the largest manager of oil and gas resources in the United States, the BLM should set the example for all oil and gas operations. BLM's rule now can join with the more responsible states in moving toward a future where the oil and gas industry develops their resources in ways that reduce threats to public health and the environment and that respect the quality of life in local communities.

Bruce Baizel
Energy Program Director
Earthworks

Improved regulation of hydraulic fracturing can reduce the risks presented by oil and gas development to clean air, clean water, wildlife habitat, and communities. Some in industry have increasingly moved to use such practices as full chemical disclosure, notice to landowners, green completions, wastewater recycling, closed-loop waste management systems, and have found that many of these approaches are economical to adopt.

III. Among state regulations, the only real consistency is variation.

In the debates over hydraulic fracturing, we often hear the argument that states are the most effective regulators, due to their understanding of local geology and their technical expertise. For many years, Earthworks has participated in various rulemaking processes and as part of governor's task forces, so we have had a chance to look carefully at the question of what makes an effective regulation. Part of the answer lies in the clear, consistent and functional statement of standards.

A survey by Resources For the Future[1] of state regulations shows the variation among the six states – California, Colorado, Montana, New Mexico, Utah, and Wyoming – in the same regulatory areas BLM addresses with this rule. For example, Montana has no requirement for intermediate or production cement casing, while Colorado requires cement casings at least 200 feet above the hydrocarbon zone. Similarly, Wyoming has a specific requirement for intermediate and production cement casings[2], while Utah has none.

Another study performed by the Ground Water Protection Council for the Environmental Defense Fund reached similar conclusions[3]. Again, looking at a number of states with a large acreage of federal lands, we find that since 2009, many states have updated their oil and gas regulations designed to protect groundwater. One of the difficulties, however, is that states have varying definitions of usable groundwater. States also have varying groundwater protection standards sometimes based on numeric levels of total dissolved solids or, alternatively, on narrative standards.

Some states have lessened the risks of ground water contamination from hydraulic fracturing by tightening their regulations in the areas of well integrity, casing, cementing, chemical disclosure, and waste disposal.

To that end, BLM commonly enters in to memoranda of understanding (MOUs) with states to help achieve better coordination. The variance procedure within the BLM hydraulic fracturing rule also fosters this type of cooperation. Rather than duplicate, the rule supplements in areas where states have yet to make important upgrades. Without this supplement, BLM would be putting all taxpayers at risk, as owners of public land and public minerals.

Conclusion

We see a need for coordinated regulation of hydraulic fracturing at all levels – federal, state and local. Based upon our experience, no single level of government can adequately regulate in a way that protects human health and our public lands, while allowing for responsible development

Bruce Baizel
Energy Program Director
Earthworks

of the resource. In times of constrained budgets and a lack of trained personnel, careful and appropriate attention by all levels of government is necessary.

The BLM rule provides a critical minimum standard for the protection of public lands and waters. It allows for greater predictability and consistency for operators. For states, it allows for the flexibility to address more individualized conditions.

We know that a significant segment of the people in the US hope that we will transition our energy mix towards renewable energy development. But, until this transition, we feel it is important to take steps to carefully regulate the oil and gas industry to minimize harm to our natural resources and public lands.

Thank you for the opportunity to present the views of Earthworks on this important topic. We appreciate the Committee's consideration of this issue and we look forward to working with you in the future to address the issue of necessary and appropriate regulation of hydraulic fracturing.

---

[1] Resources for the Future: Center for Energy, Economics, and Policy: *The State of State Shale Gas Regulation: State by State Tables* This report reviewed twenty different categories of hydraulic fracturing regulations in states with active or potential shale plays as of 2013.

[2] 200 feet above the trona interval

[3] Overview of Groundwater Protection Regulations in Oil and Gas States Steven P. Musick, P.G. Ground Water Protection Council April 2014

Senator BARRASSO. Thank you, Mr. Baizel.
Ms. Sgamma?

STATEMENT OF KATHLEEN SGAMMA, VICE PRESIDENT OF GOVERNMENT & PUBLIC AFFAIRS, WESTERN ENERGY ALLIANCE

Ms. SGAMMA. Thank you, Mr. Chairman and members of the committee.

Western Energy Alliance represents about 450 companies engaged in all aspects of environmentally responsible exploration and production of oil and natural gas in the West. Our members are proud to produce nearly a quarter of the nation's natural gas and oil production while disturbing less than a tenth of a percent of public lands.

The fundamental question related to BLM's rule before us today is whether we as a nation want to encourage the continued environmentally responsible production of oil and natural gas on public lands or do we want to shut it down. If indeed the answer is that we want to encourage the continued environmentally responsible development, then this rule is counterproductive to that goal.

I would like to make three main points: that the rule has not been properly justified; it is redundant with state regulation; and, that it cannot be efficiently implemented.

For the first point, BLM has finalized a costly rule with no justification. It can point to no single incident on Federal lands that necessitates this rule nor can it articulate one risk that is reduced because of this rule. The best BLM does to justify the rule is to cite vague notions of public concern, but are those concerns valid or just the result of misinformation and agitation? A regulator has an obligation to the regulated community and to the public to show that there is a tangible benefit for any cost, and regulatory costs affect not just the regulated industry but society at large in the form of higher energy prices, less job creation, and slower economic growth. BLM has failed in its obligation, which brings me to my next point.

Why is BLM infringing on state and tribal authority? The rule duplicates what states are already doing to protect the environment, yet BLM can show no deficiency in state regulation that would motivate this rule and it has no evidence that this costly rule will be more effective than existing state regulations. When the Federal Government feels compelled to take action that upsets the balance between States and the Federal Government, there should be a compelling reason to do so. Lack of a single incident or inability to articulate a single risk that is reduced hardly seems compelling.

In fact, BLM in the rule shows that 99.3 percent of all completions over the last couple of years were in states that have strict hydraulic fracturing regulations, and if you look at APD's approved last year, 99.97 percent are in states that have recently updated the regulations. That .3 percent represents one well in Kansas, and oh, by the way, Kansas is updating the rules as we speak.

BLM has tried to deflect criticism regarding the duplication of state regulation by suggesting that states can obtain a variance if the rules meet or exceed the requirements of the rule; however, there is no genuine mechanism in this rule for them to do so. State regulations already meet the goals of BLM's rule, yet they are not doing it in the exact prescriptive manner that BLM now demands. States are tailored to conditions on the ground, and states wisely retain flexibility to enable them to innovate and do things like more water recycling and more reuse of water, less fresh water need.

Finally, a major problem of this rule is that BLM simply does not have the resources or wherewithal to implement it. BLM petroleum engineering personnel are already spread too thin, and this rule will result in longer delays in the permitting process. Leadership at BLM has tacitly admitted this fact as they are hurrying to meet with states and try to convince them to sign MOU's. Were the rules designed to provide a genuine mechanism for granting a state variance and truly deferring to state rules, then an MOU so stating would make sense. But in the absence of such a mechanism, states are wise to refrain from entering into an MOU.

So here before us, we have a rule that is not properly justified with discernible environmental benefit. It infringes on state authority and cannot be reasonably implemented. We urge this subcommittee to pass legislation to roll back the rule.

Thank you very much.

[The prepared statement of Ms. Sgamma follows:]

Kathleen Sgamma
Vice President of Government & Public Affairs
Western Energy Alliance

Before the Senate Energy and Natural Resources Committee,
Subcommittee on Public Lands, Forests, and Mining

The Bureau of Land Management's Final Hydraulic Fracturing Rule
April 30, 2015

Chairman Barrasso, Ranking Member Wyden, and members of the committee, thank you for the opportunity to appear before you today to discuss the Bureau of Land Management's (BLM) recently finalized hydraulic fracturing rule.

Western Energy Alliance represents 450 companies engaged in all aspects of environmentally responsible exploration and production of oil and natural gas across the West. The Alliance represents independents, the majority of which are small businesses with an average of fifteen employees. Our members are proud to provide nearly a quarter of America's oil and natural gas production while disturbing only 0.07% of public lands.

The fundamental question related to BLM's final rule is whether we as a nation want to encourage responsible energy development on the vast, multiple-use public lands of the United States, or do we want to shut it down.

If the goal is to continue to discourage oil and natural gas development on federal lands, then this rule will indeed further that goal. The rule is a broad new regulatory regime with no real justification as it adds cost and delay to energy development with no identified environmental benefit; duplicates yet usurps state regulation; and cannot be implemented in an efficient manner.

If indeed the answer is that we want to encourage the continued environmentally responsible development of oil and natural gas on appropriate multiple-use public lands (i.e., non-park, non-wilderness lands), then this rule is counterproductive to that goal and should be rescinded.

Until Congress changes BLM's mandate under the Federal Land Policy and Management Act (FLPMA), BLM has a multiple-use mandate, with oil and natural gas production being a "best and proper" use of public lands. The rule before the Subcommittee today cannot realistically be addressed as furthering BLM's mandate, as another layer of redundant regulation will further discourage production of energy that all Americans own, and will continue the exit of producers from federal and tribal lands.

In addition, the Department of the Interior (DOI) owes a statutory and general trust obligation to individual Indians and tribes that are in the "best interest" of the Indian mineral owner, as embodied in the Indian Mineral Leasing Act of 1938. The Secretary of the Interior has an obligation to further the return Indian mineral owners receive from the development and production of their oil and natural gas resources. BLM's hydraulic fracturing rule runs counter to that trust obligation, as it discourages production on Indian lands. In addition, the rule is based on FLPMA, an inapplicable standard for Indian lands, and is aimed at managing Indian land resources in a manner that will protect their quality for the public at large, rather than for the benefit of Indian landowners and communities.

The actions of DOI over the last several years lead us to the conclusion that the real goal is to discourage responsible energy development on federal lands, pushing it to adjacent private and state lands or to areas of the country that are not predominated by public lands. DOI has communicated that the goal of the rule is "to support safe and responsible hydraulic fracturing on public and American Indian lands" but since development is already happening safely on federal lands, what are we to make of this and similar statements? We look at actual actions and results.

Over the last several years, DOI has enacted several policies that discourage production on federal lands. These policies include:

- "Reforms" that add years onto the leasing process, such as longer processing requirements, Master Leasing Plans, and the discontinuation of state-wide lease sales

- Land use planning restrictions more excessive than what is required to protect cultural, wildlife, land values and other resources, to the point where it becomes nearly impossible to find a time in the year where development can actually occur

- Stalled project environmental analyses under the National Environmental Policy Act (NEPA), with only three major oil and natural gas projects approved in seven years and many projects languishing in the eighth year of NEPA analysis

- Retroactive audits based on a completely new interpretation that disallows natural gas cost deductions, despite their support in statute and regulation

- Management of another 12 million acres in the Arctic National Wildlife Refuge as wilderness, despite the fact that oil and natural gas development would disturb an infinitesimal proportion of ANWR

- Initiation of a rulemaking to raise royalty, lease, civil penalty, and bonding rates.

Besides declared policies, there is deliberate bureaucratic delay. In addition to general foot dragging, BLM field offices arbitrarily add ad hoc requirements onto the permitting process at the whim of individual BLM staff and with no basis in regulation. Overall, there has been a diversion of resources from oil and natural gas to other activities, such as renewable energy development.

The results of DOI's policies are obvious. Even as production of oil and natural gas has increased dramatically across the country, it has fallen on federal lands. As the Congressional Research Service has recently reported, natural gas production has grown 37% on non-federal lands as it has decreased 31% on federal lands, and oil production has grown 89% on non-federal lands even as it has dropped 10% on federal lands and waters.

Lacks Justification

With that background, I turn to the three main points about the rule itself, starting with the fact that BLM has finalized a costly rule with no justification in the form of real environmental benefit. BLM can show no incident that necessitates the rule, nor any risk that the rule actually reduces. The best BLM can do to justify the rule is to cite vague notions of public concern. But are these concerns valid or just the result of misinformation and agitation?

A regulator has an obligation to the regulated community and the public to show that there is a tangible benefit to justify the additional cost. Regulatory costs affect not just the regulated industry, but society at large in the form of higher energy prices, fewer jobs, less government revenue, and slower economic growth. BLM has failed in its obligation and simply ignores laws that require proper justification and economic analysis, including (i) Executive Order 13563; (ii) Executive Order 12866 (Regulatory Planning and Review); (iii) the Regulatory Flexibility Act of 1980; (iv) the Small Business Regulatory Enforcement Fairness Act; and (v) the Unfunded Mandates Reform Act. For this reason, the Independent Petroleum Association of America (IPAA) and Western Energy Alliance are legally challenging the rule in the U.S. District Court of Wyoming. Wyoming, with its high proportion of federal lands and the greatest number of Applications for Permit to Drill (APD) approved every year, is the state with arguably the highest impact from this rule.

Redundant with State Regulation

That lack of justification brings me to my next point; since BLM can articulate no real reason for the rule, why is it infringing on state and tribal authority? The rule duplicates what states and tribes are already doing to protect environmental health and safety, yet BLM can show no deficiency in state regulation that would motivate it to act. BLM has no evidence that its costly proposed rule will be any more effective than existing state regulations. When the federal government feels compelled to take action that upsets the balance between states and the federal government, there should be a compelling reason to do so. Lack of a single incident or inability to articulate a single risk reduced by the rule hardly seems compelling.

In fact, BLM observes that from fiscal year 2010 to 2013 more than 99.3 percent of all well completions on federal and Indian lands occurred in nine states, all with regulations governing oil and gas development. For those states that represent that remaining .7 percent of completions on federal lands, almost all have also recently updated their oil and natural gas regulations. Looking at APDs last year, which are a good indicator of future activity affected by this rule, 99.97 percent are in states that have updated their wellbore integrity and hydraulic fracturing disclosure rules in the last few years. That number would be 100 percent except for one APD in Kansas, a state which is currently undergoing rulemaking. That percentage will likely be 100 once those wells are actually completed. I mention *recently* updated state rules, but all states with active oil and natural gas development have had wellbore integrity rules, the focus of BLM's rule, for many years if not decades.

BLM has tried to deflect criticism regarding the duplication of state regulations by suggesting that states can obtain a variance if their rules meet or exceed the requirements of the rule. Sensing vulnerability on the state issue, BLM introduced the concept of state variances between the initial rule proposed in 2012 and the second version in 2013. In the press release for the final rule, BLM states that there is a process whereby states and tribes may request variances from provisions for which they have an equal or more protective regulation in place. However, there is no genuine mechanism for state or tribal variance in the final rule. BLM has promised to work with states on Memoranda of Understanding (MOU), but those cannot substitute for a real regulatory mechanism that defers to states. BLM's rulemaking does not consider the federalism implications of BLM evaluating the adequacy of states' rules.

State regulations already meet the goals of BLM's rule, yet they are not doing so in the exact prescriptive manner that BLM now demands. State rules are tailored to the types of formations, hydrocarbon mix and composition, hydrology, topography, and other factors present in their respective state. Their rules wisely retain operation flexibility to meet the regulatory goals, instead of setting the same specific operational processes as the BLM rule dictates. These differences will not be recognized by BLM, which will instead require the exact set of requirements.

States also show leadership by allowing flexibility for operators to innovate and reduce environmental impact. Practices encouraged by states are often not possible on federal lands because of regulatory rigidity. For example, centralized fracking and gathering facilities reduce truck traffic and surface impact, yet often cannot be done on federal lands. The final BLM rule will further stifle innovation, with the tank requirements providing an example. Rigid requirements on tank size and prohibition of pits will hamper innovative centralized fluids gathering and processing that minimizes surface disturbance. Water reuse and recycling processes will be more difficult on public lands, even as adoption on non-federal lands is leading to higher levels of produced water reuse and reduced fresh water use.

Inability to Implement

Finally, a major problem of this rule is that BLM simply does not have the resources or wherewithal to implement this vast new regulatory regime. Despite a superficial economic analysis that minimized the effort to implement this rule, this rule will be difficult and costly for both industry and BLM to implement. Career BLM staff knows that petroleum engineering personnel are already spread too thin. This rule will result in ever longer delays in the permitting process. Leadership in DOI and BLM have tacitly admitted this fact, as they are hurrying to meet with states to convince them to sign onto MOUs. In effect, since BLM will not in actuality defer to state regulations, they are trying to convince the states to implement the rule for them.

Yet why should a state take up that burden? They are already meeting the overall goals of this rule, though not of course using the one-size-fits-all approach that BLM dictates. Why should the states take responsibility for implementing BLM's rule, which the federal government brought on itself without justification, when their rules more effectively achieve the same goals but in a more effective, cost-efficient manner?

Testimony of Kathleen Sgamma

Page 5 of 5

Were the rule designed to provide a genuine mechanism for granting a state a variance and truly deferring to state rules, then an MOU so stating would make sense. But in the absence of such a mechanism, states are wise to refrain from entering into an MOU to implement this poorly conceived rule. In fact, Wyoming, North Dakota and Colorado are challenging the legality of the rule in the U.S. District Court in Wyoming.

So here before us we have a rule that is not properly justified, delivers no discernable environmental benefit, infringes on state authority, and cannot be reasonably implemented. Yet BLM is rushing to implement this rule by June 24th. Having taken over four years to write the final rule, BLM now rushes to implement it in only three months. That is not a realistic timeframe, and IPAA and Western Energy Alliance are seeking a preliminary injunction to stay its implementation. We urge this Subcommittee and Congress to advance legislation to roll back the rule and instead grant state and tribal regulation primacy on oil and natural gas development, including hydraulic fracturing.

Kathleen Sgamma

Senator BARRASSO. Thank you very much, Ms. Sgamma.
Mr. Watson?

STATEMENT OF MARK WATSON, STATE OIL AND GAS SUPER-VISOR, WYOMING OIL AND GAS CONSERVATION COMMISSION

Mr. WATSON. Thank you, Chairman Barrasso and members of the committee.

Wyoming was one of the first states to implement comprehensive rules on hydraulic fracturing, or fracking, and these rules have been enforced on all State, private, and Federal minerals since 2010. We were the first state to require disclosure of all chemicals used in the fracking process prior to issuing a permit. In fact, Secretary of the Interior Sally Jewell often cites Wyoming's rules on fracking as a standard for other states to follow. Our rules governing wellbore integrity and water management have been in place for decades and are updated as new technologies become commonplace in the energy industry. Wyoming's new baseline water quality rule, which requires testing of offsite water wells before and after the drilling of a well, and air quality rules in the Pinedale area are but a few of the many examples of Wyoming's progressive approach to rulemaking.

Recently the Bureau of Land Management announced a new rule on fracking. Not only does this rule come late, it adopts the one-size-fits-all approach. It creates confusion and bureaucracy in an already complex process. It will inevitably lead to delays in the permitting process for operators without increasing environmental protection or providing more information for the public to review.

Wyoming maintains public access to the fracking plans, which include all the chemicals used, as well as pre-and post-reporting on fracking operations, in its files and electronically on its website. All the information collected on fracking operations is available to the public, to industry, and to other regulators for use in reviewing best management practices, determining fracking impacts to offset wells, or even for a homeowner who wants to know what is going on at the well near their home.

Despite Mr. Kornze's testimony, the BLM frack rule has no current method to provide any information on a publicly-available website other than the post-fracking operations chemical disclosure reported to FracFocus. While reporting the chemical information to FracFocus or another publicly available data base is vital, reviewing other details concerning the fracking operations can be just as important. It would be very difficult for anyone outside of the BLM staff to review information related to cement quality, well integrity, injection pressures, etcetera using the current information systems employed by the BLM. All this data is readily available on our website for public viewing.

In its response to comments under federalism assessment, the BLM noted that they do not believe that production from Federal lands will be reduced and therefore no financial impacts would occur to states as a result of the new fracking rule. Currently in Wyoming, 54 percent of our oil production and 76 percent of gas production comes from Federal minerals. To make a statement that the new fracking rule will not impact states such as Wyoming is simply wrong. Currently Wyoming's average time for processing a drilling permit is 60 days while the BLM processing time is 200 days. Further delays will occur with the BLM using the same staff that approves drilling permits to now also approve fracking operations. The practice of horizontal well drilling further complicates the approval of fracking operations. More of the proposed wells in Wyoming are encountering a combination of minerals by drilling through and producing from a mixture of Federal, fee, and State minerals. The uncertainty and potentially long wait times for BLM approval of fracking operations will act as encouragement for operators to exclude the Federal minerals from the planned well. This will potentially strand the Federal minerals, leaving them out of the production of the well and thus creating waste. There have already been several cases of Federal minerals being excluded from drilling and spacing units that have been approved by my agency due to the length of time it takes for a BLM permit to be approved. The additional delays for approval of fracking operations by the BLM will clearly provide a disincentive to develop production on Federal minerals.

In comments to the Federal fracking rule, several states, including Wyoming, requested exemptions for those states that already had comprehensive frack rules in place. The BLM, in an attempt to address those concerns, included a section in the final rule allowing for states to apply for a variance for all wells within the state. However, upon further review and meetings with BLM officials in Wyoming, it became apparent that the variance was simply a requirement that allowed the BLM to require additional information if the state's requirements exceeded those objectives of the BLM frack rule. In other words, it was a variance for the Federal Government; the goal being that both the state and the BLM would receive the same package of information. This is clearly a duplication of effort that forces operators to comply with two regulatory agencies. The Wyoming Oil and Gas Conservation Commission has one office versus the BLM who has nine field offices in Wyoming, which can lead to varying interpretations when implementing the new frack rule. This creates confusion and uncertainty and leads to unnecessary delays in the permitting process.

A better solution would be a mechanism to allow states to apply for primacy if they could demonstrate that the objectives of the BLM frack rule could be met by the states' rules and regulations. This would provide certainty and uniformity in enforcing a frack rule for the benefit of citizens and the oil and gas industry. The Underground Injection Control Program, a program that regulates injection wells, is a prime example of a Federal rule that is implemented and enforced by the states.

In conclusion, Wyoming believes that the states are best positioned to regulate hydraulic fracturing. Wyoming has successfully imposed its hydraulic fracturing rule on Federal, State, and private minerals for five years and has an experienced and qualified staff to enforce these rules.

This concludes my oral testimony. Thank you.

[The prepared statement of Mr. Watson follows:]

Mark Watson

State Oil and Gas Supervisor

Wyoming Oil and Gas Conservation Commission

Thank you. Chairman Barrasso and members of the committee, my name is Mark Watson and I am the Oil and Gas Supervisor for the Wyoming Oil and Gas Conservation Commission.

Wyoming was one of the first states to implement comprehensive rules on hydraulic fracturing, or fracking, and these rules have been enforced on all state, private and federal minerals since 2010. We were the first state to require disclosure of all chemicals used in the fracking process prior to issuing a permit. In fact, Secretary of the Interior Sally Jewel often cites Wyoming's rules on fracking as a standard for other states to follow. Our rules governing wellbore integrity and water management have been in place for decades and are updated as new technologies become commonplace in the energy industry. Wyoming's new baseline water quality rule, which requires testing of offset water wells before and after the drilling of a well, and air quality rules in the Pinedale area are a few of the many examples of Wyoming's progressive approach to rulemaking.

Recently the Bureau of Land Management (BLM) announced a new rule on fracking. Not only does this rule come late, it adopts a one-size-fits-all approach. It creates confusion and bureaucracy in an already complex process. It will inevitably lead to delays in the permitting process for operators without increasing environmental protection or providing more information for the public to review.

Wyoming maintains public access to the fracking plans including pre and post reporting on fracking operations in its files and electronically on its website. All information collected on fracking operations is available to the public, to industry, and to regulators for use in reviewing best management practices, determining fracking impacts to offset wells, or even to a homeowner who wants to know what is going on at the well near their home. The BLM frack rule has no current method to provide any information on a publically available website other than post fracking operations chemical disclosure reported to FracFocus. While reporting the chemical information to FracFocus or another publicly available database is vital, reviewing other details concerning the fracking operations can be just as important. It would be very difficult for anyone outside of BLM staff to review information related to cement quality, well integrity, injection pressures, etc. using current information systems employed by the BLM. All this data is readily available on our website for public viewing.

In its response to comments under federalism assessment, the BLM noted that they do not believe that production from federal lands will be reduced and therefore no financial impacts would occur to states as a result of the new fracking rule. Currently in Wyoming, 54% of oil production and 76% of gas production comes from federal minerals. To make a statement that the new fracking rule will not impact states such as Wyoming is simply wrong. Currently, Wyoming's average time for processing a drilling permit is 60 days while the BLM processing time is in excess of 200 days. Further delays will occur with the BLM using the same staff that approves drilling permits to also approve fracking operations. The practice of horizontal well drilling further complicates the approval of fracking operations. More of the proposed wells in Wyoming are encountering a combination of minerals by drilling through and producing from a mix of federal, fee, and state minerals. The uncertainty and potentially long wait times for BLM approval of fracking operations will act as encouragement for operators to exclude the federal minerals from the planned well. This will potentially strand the federal minerals, leaving them out of the production of the well and creating waste. There have already been several cases of federal minerals being excluded from drilling and spacing units that have been approved by the Wyoming Oil and Gas Conservation Commission due to the length of time it takes the BLM to approve an APD. The additional delays for approval of fracking operations by the BLM will clearly provide a disincentive to develop production on federal minerals.

In comments to the federal fracking rule, several states, including Wyoming, requested exemptions for those states that already had comprehensive frack rules in place. The BLM, in an attempt to address those concerns, included a section in the final rule allowing for states to apply for a variance for all wells within a state. However, upon further review and meetings with BLM officials, it became apparent that the variance was simply a requirement that allowed the BLM to require additional information if the states requirements exceeded those objectives of the BLM frack rule. The goal being that both the state and the BLM would receive the same package of information. This is clearly a duplication of effort that forces operators to comply with two regulatory agencies. The Wyoming Oil and Gas Conservation Commission has one office versus the BLM who has nine field offices in Wyoming, which could lead to varying interpretations when implementing the new frack rule. This creates confusion and uncertainty and leads to unnecessary delays in the permitting process.

A better solution would be a mechanism to allow states to apply for primacy if they could demonstrate that the objectives of the BLM frack rule could be met by the states rules and regulations. This would provide certainty and uniformity in enforcing a frack rule for the benefit of citizens and the oil and gas industry. The Underground Injection Control Program, a program that regulates injection wells, is a prime example of a federal rule that is implemented and enforced by the states.

In conclusion, Wyoming believes that the states are best positioned to regulate hydraulic fracturing. Wyoming has successfully imposed its hydraulic fracturing rule on federal, state and private minerals for five years and has an experienced and qualified staff to enforce these rules.

This concludes my oral testimony.

Senator BARRASSO. Thank you very much, Mr. Watson.

Some of the members have questions, and we will start with Senator Capito.

Senator CAPITO. Thank you, Mr. Chairman, and I appreciate all of our witnesses today.

I wanted to followup with Mr. Kornze. Some of the comments that were made by Ms. Sgamma. She mentioned in her presentation that you had not identified a single environmental problem related, you had not had a single incident that your rule was trying to help or an incident that had happened. The question it raised in my mind is, have you uncovered any new or previously unknown environmental problems or incidents that your rule would fix which are not addressed by state laws that you could share with us today?

Mr. KORNZE. So the goal of the rule is to address the same issues that state regulators are addressing but to do it on a nationwide basis, and part of the important point here is that the Bureau of Land Management has responsibility for oil and gas leases in 32 different states. There are some states who have done an excellent job in this area. Not all states have been as advanced as states like Wyoming, for instance.

So related to sort of the purpose of stepping forward on this, the same need that the states saw is the same need that we see, which is you have much more sophisticated drilling techniques being used. You have very intense pressures, a whole different scale of pressure being applied to these wells than 10, 30, 40 years ago when a lot of our regulations were put in place. And so the same quality standards that the states see a necessity to bring forward new regulation is what has also been driving our efforts.

Senator CAPITO. But the base question I was asking was is there an incident? Has something prompted this in more recent history?

Mr. KORNZE. No single incident, no.

Senator CAPITO. Let me ask a question about something that Mr. Watson mentioned in his opening statement. He mentioned transparency, and I think this has been an issue in West Virginia. Transparency was one of the issues that the state legislature tried to address. He mentioned that all of the chemicals and all of the information is there basically in real time. Is that basically the interpretation I had, Mr. Watson, of what is going on?

Mr. WATSON. As far as the BLM website?

Senator CAPITO. No, your website.

Mr. WATSON. Oh, yes. Our website has all the information, not just the chemicals.

Senator CAPITO. But you said that your understanding of the BLM rule would be that theirs would not be as transparent as what you have at the state right now. Is that correct?

Mr. WATSON. That is correct.

Senator CAPITO. Do you have a response to that?

Mr. KORNZE. Yes, I found that to be an interesting point. That actually is something that we are very interested in. We have what I think we would broadly recognize as a very old system. So we are still using paper files in most offices, and so we have a very strong desire to step forward. One thing we are working on right now is catching up states like Colorado in terms of with our drilling permit application. We are making an effort hopefully by the end of this year to go online nationwide so that you can submit your drilling permit application electronically. You can know where we are at in the processing, and that we can hopefully provide better online information so you can have the kind of transparency that Wyoming has.

Senator CAPITO. I think this points to a good illustration in that the State of Wyoming is so much more forward-leaning than what you have just described at the BLM. Why not cede to the State of Wyoming this transparency and let them have the state primacy over this? Because they do have a system that is fully developed and fully fleshed out. That is what I do not understand.

Mr. KORNZE. This goes back to my initial offering that we have responsibilities nationwide, and so what we have tried to build in this rule is something that provides a basic foundation. I think the operators that are working in Wyoming are going to have no problem following the rule that BLM has laid out because it is very similar to what Wyoming has in place.

So what we developed, the variance process, which has been discussed a little bit, to make sure that as has been the case for many, many years, when there are Federal rules in place and State rules in place, the higher standard is followed and everyone carries forward. And so this is the way that oil and gas has worked and this is the way that we have worked together as a Federal Government and as states for ages. And so there is nothing fundamentally different about this rule and about how it will work. So we have got a baseline, and I think we are excited to work closely with states like Wyoming.

Senator CAPITO. Mr. Watson, is that how you see this rule in terms of working State/Federal? You basically said you have been working like this anyway, and it is going to have very little impact in Wyoming.

Mr. WATSON. Well, that is not true as far as fracking because the BLM has not imposed any fracking rules. So for the last five years, we have imposed our rule on Federal lands.

Senator CAPITO. All right, thank you.

Senator BARRASSO. Thank you, Senator Capito.

Next, Senator Daines.

Senator DAINES. Thank you, Mr. Chairman.

Kind of building on where Senator Capito was going there, I guess I just heard there was not an incident that triggered these additional regulations. Is that right, Mr. Kornze?

Mr. KORNZE. That is correct.

Senator DAINES. Furthermore, I have just heard states like Wyoming, Colorado—I know there are others—are actually ahead in terms of their systems processes and so forth than even the BLM processes. Is that correct?

Mr. KORNZE. In some cases, that is true.

Senator DAINES. We in Montana updated our hydraulic fracturing rules in 2011. In fact, we have some of the most robust chemical disclosure rules in the country. What would I tell a Montanan right now and say why the Federal Government knows better than we in the state? What do I tell a Montanan right now when we have state-of-the-art regulations in place? It is working beautifully. We have got to drink the water, breathe the air, recreate on these lands. It is close to us. We want to preserve and protect it. What do I tell a Montanan around why the BLM can come in and tell us a better way to do it?

Mr. KORNZE. So without knowing the—I mean, we would want to sit down and look side-by-side in terms of if there are differences. My guess would be if you do have one of the most forward-leaning disclosure rules in the country, that our rule will not change the standards that you have to follow. So I think what you would tell a Montanan is the Federal Government, which has responsibility to a nationwide regulated community, all Americans, has made sure that the standards we have—that there is a similar standard nationwide to what we have done in Montana. So we in Montana can be proud——

Senator DAINES. But also we pay a lot of Federal taxes as well. I think they would ask themselves what are we getting for our return investment of having Federal hours and tax dollars spent with the redundancy arguably putting regulations in place that are even backward-looking versus states that really have forward-looking, state-of-the-art regs?

Mr. KORNZE. Well, I think it is important to understand how oil and gas regulations work. So this goes back to the States and the Federal Government working together. So I think the gentleman from Wyoming said that has not been the case in hydraulic fracturing because BLM has not had a modern rule. We had one in the early 1980's but had to be revised to sort of catch up to modern practice, which is what we have done. But in all other areas, since 1981, the Bureau of Land Management has updated 37 different oil and gas regulations. So to us updating and in a dance on this nationwide scale with states is nothing new. Some states are ahead of us, some states are behind us, and this is how the process has rolled forward.

But I think for your Montanan, you can say, hey, look, this is not an onerous rule. This is a common sense rule that dovetails well with what we have and——

Senator DAINES. Well, I can tell you most Montanans—when the Federal Government comes in and says this is not going to be an onerous rule, we do not believe it. It is based on our experience.

I guess this really leads me to another question, which is just geological differences and so forth there across the country, as we look at hydraulic fracturing. Can you help me understand the thought process of BLM when this rule is designed without application to legacy shallow gas wells and conventional fields?

Mr. KORNZE. Can you restate the question?

Senator DAINES. So the rule did not take into account the application of legacy shallow gas wells and conventional fields.

Mr. KORNZE. Well, anyone that drills a well after June 24th, I believe the day is, will have to follow this if they are using hydraulic fracturing. So it applies——

Senator DAINES. I thought there was an exception for the rule for shallow gas wells.

Mr. KORNZE. Not that I am aware of. If I am incorrect, I will come back to you.

Senator DAINES. Okay, because more than half the wells in Montana will need exception to that rule. So I am just concerned this approach is a one-size-fits-all when clearly just looking at geology, there is a lot of difference between deep and shallow wells.

How many years has the BLM been working on this rule?

Mr. KORNZE. I believe—well, Secretary Salazar held a forum in I believe it was October 2010—October or November.

Senator DAINES. So it has been about five years, roughly.

Now, I am understanding the rule needs to be implemented less than 90 days after it was released in March. Is that correct?

Mr. KORNZE. That is true. And by law, we are only required 60 days. We extended 30 additional days because we were doing outreach with industry and with states and making sure that we have more time.

Senator DAINES. If it was a five-year process to develop the rule, is there a reason you are only giving the states less than 90 days for enforceability?

Mr. KORNZE. Well, I will tell you throughout this process I am proud of the outreach that we have done and the coordination with states. I have spent time in Denver sitting down with the State of Wyoming's regulators, the State of Colorado's regulators, with Utah, with tribes. I have gone to reservations in North Dakota to sit down with tribal members and tribal regulators to understand how they are approaching this. So I think we have been robust in our engagement. We actually took the unusual step of having two different draft rules. So we had one in 2012 and I believe one——

Senator DAINES. But the states will have less than 90 days before they must enforce the rules. Is that right?

Mr. KORNZE. And I appreciate you are trying to get me to answer. So the point is we have had a long, collaborative conversation on this, and so there should not be any surprises.

Senator DAINES. I am out of time. Mr. Chairman, thank you.

Senator BARRASSO. Thank you, Senator Daines.

Senator Lee?

Senator LEE. Thank you, Mr. Chairman.

Mr. Kornze, you mentioned a minute ago that some states were better than others in their existing regulations of hydraulic fracturing. What can you tell me about what issues you might have found in Utah? Were there issues with Utah's regulations that you found inadequate, and if so, what were those?

Mr. KORNZE. I appreciate the question, Senator Lee.

As we worked on this and we sat down with state regulators, with industry, with environmental organizations, with the general public, what we were looking at is what are the best management practices. So we did not necessarily take it upon ourselves to sort of say Utah is good or bad or Kansas is good or bad. We tried to look at where is this leaning, where is it now, what are the best practices.

Senator LEE. So it was not necessarily the case that any state was inadequate.

Mr. KORNZE. No.

Senator LEE. And if no state was inadequate, then why was it necessary to come up with a national standard particularly in light of the geology that differs from one state to another?

Mr. KORNZE. Well, I will tell you that only roughly half of the states that we have oil and gas leases in that we have oversight responsibility for have stepped forward and regulated in this area of hydraulic fracturing.

Senator LEE. Okay. But of those states, you have not found any to be inadequate in their regulation?

Mr. KORNZE. Well, I am saying we have not taken it upon ourselves to make that kind of judgment. So that was not the approach that we took. But roughly half of the states that we regulate in have not stepped forward to regulate in this area.

Senator LEE. Okay.

Mr. KORNZE. So our standards that we have just put forward would be the baseline standards on public lands. There otherwise would not be standards on those Federal lands.

Senator LEE. Okay, so that is a good point. If that is the case, if you have got a number of states that do not have any regulations at all and you have got other states that do have regulations, none of which are inadequate, why not allow those states that have regulations that you have now acknowledged are adequate to remain in effect rather than being replaced by a national rule?

Mr. KORNZE. So that comes to the variance process and how oil and gas has worked in terms of regulation. So if the State of Utah historically has had basic standards for, let us say, disposal of water or basic drilling techniques, those would be laid against the standards that the Bureau of Land Management has put forward for Federal lands, and our regulators would work together in the field, and they would say which standard is higher, more restrictive, and that standard would apply. So if Utah had exceeded BLM standards in a certain area, we would be following Utah's standards on public lands.

Senator LEE. Will this not inevitably extend the period of time that it takes to get regulatory approval, given that the rule contemplates a need to either get this approval from BLM as part of the APD process or outside the process separately? Now, in my state, in Utah, it already takes about 200 days to get an APD approved. Do you think it is reasonable to expect BLM field staff to take on this added responsibility of approving these fracking permits and to not expect additional delays in the process?

Mr. KORNZE. So we have looked at this, and I believe this is spoken to in the rule that we expect the additional workload on our end is about four hours per drilling application. So there is additional information that we are going to be looking at. So is there an increase? Yes. Is it significant? We do not see it as such. Do I think that 200 days is a great number? I do not. And so we are working aggressively to see what we can do to bring that down. We were at 300 days a few years ago. I am proud that we have made this progress. And this online permitting system that I mentioned earlier, I think, is really going to help us step forward and hopefully make some system changes that will help permitting times across the country.

Senator LEE. Okay.

I want to get back to the state-by-state issue we talked about a minute ago. If the rule allows for variances, is that not basically what we were already doing under the process that utilized memoranda of understanding? In the case of Utah, for example, there was a memorandum of understanding that had just recently been entered into. So in light of that, why not just respect the MOU? Why not just honor the MOU and allow that to stand?

Mr. KORNZE. So the MOU's are very helpful and important. It was mentioned earlier in another witness' testimony about what these are. And I tell you we have been reaching out to states sort of since I got involved in the Bureau of Land Management's oil and gas program. The efficiencies that are possible through these MOU's, making sure that—let us say, for instance, in a big state like yours that there is one state well down by Kanab, but we have 100, and vice versa up in Box Elder County, we have got two and you guys have got 50. We can sort of have resource sharing and workload sharing that can make a big difference. So that is the point of some of the MOU's, but also we can use those MOU's to codify an understanding of what kind of variances might be allowable between State rules and Federal rules. So we have had these conversations.

So the MOU you spoke to is partially focused on efficiency of working together, but the MOU's we are talking about today in the context of a variance would be more specific to these rules. So because we now have a rule, that is what prompts the conversation and hopefully the updating of that MOU.

Senator LEE. Thank you for your answers. I appreciate your testimony and your hard work on this, but my time has expired.

I do want to state for the record I have got concerns. This appears to me to be something that could well be a solution in search of a problem. I have not heard testimony today indicating a single problem with a single state's regulation of hydraulic fracturing. Not a single one. In light of that, I struggle a lot with the idea that we need a new national regulatory scheme.

Thank you, Mr. Chairman.

Senator BARRASSO. Thank you, Senator Lee.

Senator Daines, would you like to go with another round of questioning? Go right ahead.

Senator DAINES. Thank you, Mr. Chairman.

I just want to go back on that shallow well issue and clarify. Our understanding is there is no exception for shallow wells written in the rule, but we have been told by field staff that they would have to give exception to shallow wells. Is that your understanding?

Mr. KORNZE. I have not read into the specific issue, so if I could followup with you after the hearing.

Senator DAINES. Well, that is what we have been hearing back in Montana, and the point is about half of the 800 wells in Montana are shallow wells.

Mr. KORNZE. Are these coalbed methane wells? Is that what you are talking about?

Senator DAINES. They call them shallow legacy wells. They would likely receive an exemption, but we would have to make that application for it. So it, again, just looks like, as Senator Lee mentioned, it is a solution in search of a problem right now.

I want to turn to Ms. Sgamma. In the BLM rule, it says it will actually facilitate oil and gas development. Do you believe it will speed up, facilitate development of Federal lands?

Ms. SGAMMA. Well, adding more Federal regulation and red tape rarely does speed things up.

I think BLM has minimized the implementation of this rule. I think they have minimized both the cost and the effort. There is an entirely new decision point that is in this rule that requires engineering staff at BLM to make determinations on things. And if there are certain readings, certain pressure testing readings—and probably Mr. Watson can explain that better, but there are things that BLM has to be notified of and may require an operator to wait until an answer comes back from BLM. And there is nothing in the rule that requires BLM to respond in a certain amount of time. So we just do not see how this rule can be easily implemented.

Four hours of staff time when you have got additional engineering information that has to be gone through, decision points on whether the hydraulic fracturing process can go forward, and then of course, on industry's side, this is not a simple rule to enforce. It is not just a matter of, oh, we are already doing it anyway. An operator could be already voluntarily doing most of the things in this rule, but the additional paperwork requirements and the additional information that must be supplied will just by necessity take additional staff time.

Senator DAINES. So continuing on that line of thinking, the Administration has proposed increased royalty fees and other fees for oil and gas on Federal lands. Will increasing royalty fees on Federal lands in your opinion facilitate or deter oil and gas development?

Ms. SGAMMA. Well, it will continue the exodus off of Federal lands and onto adjacent private and State lands, or what happens a lot is producers move from states in the West predominated by Federal lands like Montana and Wyoming and other areas of the country where they do not have that additional red tape. You know, the Interior Department has chosen to take more resources from industry in the form of additional regulation. And you know, it takes years longer not just at the permitting stage but at every stage from leasing to environmental analysis to the permitting stage to get a project approved and completed.

Senator DAINES. So if the exploration moves completely off of Federal lands, what does that mean to the taxpayer?

Ms. SGAMMA. The taxpayer will get much less revenue return, and we have seen revenue onshore go down over the last several years.

Senator DAINES. Director Kornze, I want to go back to the discussion about tribes, and I appreciate the outreach you have had to tribes. Back in Montana, we believe that our tribes should have the freedom to develop their own natural resources if they choose especially due to the high unemployment rates that we see, oftentimes in excess of 50 percent, and the need for essential services in their communities. Yet, it is my understanding that some tribes have expressed concerns about the BLM's proposed rule.

Director, can you expand on the tribal consultation process that BLM underwent with Indian tribes on this final rule?

Mr. KORNZE. We have been consulting with tribes throughout the process. We had a very significant collaboration and consultation process during the drafting and during the comment periods

around that. And so that was part of my visit to the Three Affili-
ated Tribes, was we were holding regional tribal conversation
where many tribes from Montana attended.

Senator DAINES. With all of that input that you received, how
many changes to the final rule occurred to accommodate the tribe's
concerns?

Mr. KORNZE. I am sorry.

Senator DAINES. With all the input you received from the tribes,
how many changes occurred to the final rule to accommodate their
concerns?

Mr. KORNZE. I could not give you a strict number, but I can tell
you that tribal input did have an imprint on this bill and you can
see it in what we developed.

Senator DAINES. Just maybe as a followup, it would be helpful
to get the specific changes made to the rule as a result of the input
the tribes gave this process.

Mr. KORNZE. We should be able to provide that to you.

Senator DAINES. All right, thank you.

Thanks, Mr. Chairman.

Senator BARRASSO. Thank you much, Senator Daines.

Mr. Kornze, BLM received public comments urging your agency
to examine the impacts that the hydraulic fracturing rule was
going to have on states. The comments called on the BLM to conduct what is known as a federalism assessment under Executive
Order 13132. BLM responded to the comments in its final rule. The
final rule says the BLM believes that there will be no financial impacts to the states as a result of this rule. It goes on to say that
the BLM does not believe that production from Federal lands will
be reduced as a result of this rule. Therefore, a federalism assessment, it says, is not required. Did the BLM rely on any empirical
data to show that a rule of this significance would not reduce oil
and gas production on Federal lands?

Mr. KORNZE. We can provide you an answer on the federalism
assessment. That is a fairly specific corner of the rule, but we
would be happy to get back to you on that.

Senator BARRASSO. We would like for you to submit any data
that you used, as part of the hearing record, because we are just
trying to figure out the basis of BLM's statement that the rule will
not reduce oil and gas production on Federal lands. For most of us,
we think that is hard to believe and we are trying to figure out
what helped you come to that conclusion.

Mr. KORNZE. If you do not mind me taking a second, I do think
there is an interesting narrative that Federal regulation drives
away investment. We have places like in the Marcellus shale where
there is an abundance of natural gas opportunity but also significant infrastructure. So we have seen development of natural gas
move to areas like that and in places like Wyoming that are rich
in natural gas, there has been a decline. But it does not mean that
those resources will not be developed when there is more resource.
I think it is more the market reacting to whatever is happening
today.

But there is also an interesting counter-example where if you
look at where BLM rules apply, they apply to both public lands and
to tribal lands. And on tribal lands during this Administration

there has been an almost 500 percent increase in oil production. And so that is under the rules the Federal Government has. We have seen an almost 500 percent increase, and so I think that tells a story of where there is significant opportunity, you will see significant production.

Senator BARRASSO. I would say as Chairman of the Indian Affairs Committee, 500 percent could be five times the amount of a very little amount, just a little bit more, because we continue to hear significant stories of inability of the Indian tribes and on Indian reservations opportunities to actually use the resources because of additional impact of Federal regulations making it that much harder to use significant amounts of resources that are there.

Mr. Watson, you have been 31 years on the Wyoming Oil and Gas Conservation Commission. Do you believe that this rule is going to have a negative impact on oil and gas production on Federal lands?

Mr. WATSON. Oh, it definitely will, and I have already seen it with the delay in permitting.

Senator BARRASSO. Ms. Sgamma, what are your views on the same thing? With all your experience, do you believe the rule will negatively impact oil and gas production on Federal lands?

Ms. SGAMMA. Absolutely. You know, there are just so many additional requirements on Federal lands and so many different policies that have been put in place over the last several years that are slowing development on Federal lands and just making it more difficult. Our members continually tell us that they avoid at all costs Federal lands.

Senator BARRASSO. In an answer to a previous question, you said something about you hardly ever see a situation where more red tape and regulations make things actually easier. If you could actually find any time that they have made things easier, if you could submit that for the record, I think that would be—— [Laughter.]

Ms. SGAMMA. I will do some research.

Senator BARRASSO. Thank you. Do not waste a lot of time, though. Thank you.

Mr. Watson, in your testimony, you discussed the variance process. I understand that a state may apply for a variance if a state's own hydraulic fracturing rule meets or exceeds the objective of the BLM's rule. You explained that a variance does not give a state authority to enforce its own rules on Federal lands. Instead, a variance allows the BLM to apply alternative or additional regulations to its final rule. This brings a whole new meaning to the phrase "no good deed goes unpunished."

So if your understanding of a variance is correct, does the State of Wyoming have any incentive to obtain a variance?

Mr. WATSON. Not for Wyoming. There would be no incentive at all.

Senator BARRASSO. So, Mr. Kornze, would you like to comment on that?

Mr. KORNZE. You know, the State of Wyoming and the Bureau of Land Management are in the midst of discussions, and so the reports I have gotten out of that are general in nature, but there is a sense that they have been productive and that Wyoming is pursuing these conversations in potential pursuit of a variance.

Senator BARRASSO. Mr. Watson, I understand the oil and gas producers in Wyoming are already taking steps to avoid Federal oil and gas. Specifically, oil and gas producers are establishing what are known as spacing units which include private and State lands but exclude Federal land. Would you discuss this at greater length for the committee?

Mr. WATSON. So a spacing unit just defines the area that one well will drain and it includes Federal, State, and fee. So we see a lot in the examiner hearings, which I have done a lot of, where the actual wellbore at one point there will be Federal lands, and they will just cut that out. So basically we call it spacing them out, or for instance, the east half might be Federal. The west half is fee. They will just space the west half and just leave the Feds out. So I see that all the time.

Senator BARRASSO. Ms. Sgamma, in your testimony, you tell us the actions of the Department of the Interior over the last several years lead us to the conclusion that the real goal is to discourage responsible energy development on Federal lands, pushing it to adjacent private and State lands or to areas of the country that are not predominated by public lands.

Would you please expand upon your comments for the committee?

Ms. SGAMMA. We have just seen several policies that really are not furthering the goal of more oil and natural gas development on Federal lands. I mean, I think we can all agree that we want them done in a environmentally responsible manner. We feel that we have achieved a balance by providing quite a large energy resource while disturbing a small percentage of public lands. So some of the policies include leasing reforms that have added additional layers of NEPA and additional delays in the leasing process. We have seen land use planning restrictions and resource management plan amendments that leave us scratching our heads trying to think how we can possibly operate in areas when there are so many overlaying regulations. You cannot even find a month in a year that there is not something that is keeping you off development, and those are going to get worse when the sage grouse amendments come out. We have seen stalled project environmental analysis. There are several projects in Wyoming, for example, that are in the eighth year and there is just no end in sight or no plan for moving those NEPA documents.

Recently we have seen very hostile, retroactive audits based on new interpretations of the regulations, and we have seen things like more acreage being put off. I mean, the latest example is in the Arctic National Wildlife Refuge where 12 million acres is not going to be considered for oil and gas development.

And now, as you mentioned, we have got a new rulemaking process on increasing the royalty rate. I mean, when you have already made it so much more expensive to operate on Federal lands and your breakeven point is so much higher on Federal lands because of all of the additional costs, raising the royalty rate simply will make a lot of development uneconomic.

Senator BARRASSO. Thank you.

Mr. Kornze, I understand the BLM examined state hydraulic fracturing regulations as it developed its final rule. BLM reviewed existing regulations in Wyoming, as well as California, Colorado, Montana, New Mexico, North Dakota, Oklahoma, Texas, and Utah. According to BLM, these states accounted for 99.3 percent of the total oil and gas wells completed on Federal and Indian lands from 2010 to 2013.

Do you know which, if any, of these states have actually failed to regulate hydraulic fracturing in a sufficient manner?

Mr. KORNZE. Well, as noted earlier, we were looking for best practices. We have 32 different states that have oil and gas leases that we have oversight responsibility for, and so we drew from many sources, including many states like the ones you mentioned, for those best management practices to lay down a basic common sense standard that should apply nationwide wherever Federal lands are drilled on.

Senator BARRASSO. Well, I think it is disappointing to people here who are listening in on this that we cannot really get an answer to the question from the Administration of which of these states does not measure up. It does not seem that the Administration can find fault in the state hydraulic fracturing regulations of any of these states. That to me says that the BLM's final rule is redundant and unnecessary. I think that is the kind of a thing that Senator Lee made reference to of a solution in search of a problem.

I do have one additional question. The BLM has not yet issued a final environmental impact statement for an oil and gas project in Wyoming since 2008, and it is now 2015. So BLM has not issued a final environmental impact statement for an oil and gas project in Wyoming since 2008. Currently there nine environmental impact statements for oil and gas projects in Wyoming pending with BLM. I know you have not been there the whole time. I am well aware of that. Some of these impact statements have been pending with BLM for eight years. I think it is inexcusable for any Federal agency to be in that situation.

Do you have any idea when we can expect BLM to issue some of these final environmental impact statements for these projects?

Mr. KORNZE. So I am glad you asked this question. The Governor's office has raised the same issue with me, so I have looked into it. We do have those nine projects that are moving forward. About half of those came in in the last two years.

One of the exciting things about Wyoming in the oil and gas realm on public lands is we have 100,000 wells nationwide that we have oversight responsibility for right now. There are almost 40,000 that are going to come online through these nine EIS's just in Wyoming alone. So we are very much leaning forward into the process. The Continental Divide-Creston is probably going to be the first one to come through that system. So we expect some progress on that and one or two other major EIS's this year that will speak to thousands and thousands of additional wells in Wyoming.

Senator BARRASSO. Well, thank you.

Ms. Sgamma, do you see these sorts of delays in other states?

Ms. SGAMMA. Utah. Utah is the other state with several projects being held up.

Senator BARRASSO. Thank you.

Without any other members here, I appreciate each of you being here today to testify, to share your insights.

The hearing record will stay open for two weeks. Some of the other members of the committee who were not able to be here today may supply additional questions in writing, and I would hope that you would be able to get back to them with answers in a timely manner. Thank you.

With that, this hearing is adjourned.

[Whereupon, at 3:31 p.m., the hearing was adjourned.]

APPENDIX MATERIAL SUBMITTED

U.S. Senate Committee on Energy and Natural Resources
April 30, 2015 Hearing: BLM Hydraulic Fracturing Rule
Questions for the Record Submitted to the Honorable Neil Kornze

Questions from Senator John Barrasso

Question 1: The Bureau of Land Management's final rule on hydraulic fracturing says that: "The BLM believes that there will be no financial impacts to the states as a result of this rule." It goes on to say that: "the BLM does not believe that production from Federal lands will be reduced as a result of this rule. Therefore, a Federalism assessment is not required." At the hearing, I asked you: (1) whether BLM relied on any empirical data to show that a rule of this significance would not reduce oil and gas production on federal lands; and (2) if BLM did not rely on empirical data, what is the basis for BLM's finding that the rule will not reduce oil and gas production on federal lands?

In response, you indicated that you would provide a written answer to this question. I look forward to your answer.

Response:

Consistent with applicable legal requirements, the Bureau of Land Management (BLM) published a Regulatory Impact Analysis (RIA) for the hydraulic fracturing rule on March 26, 2015, concurrent with the rule. The RIA compares the industry's costs of compliance with the requirements of the final rule, with the costs for drilling and hydraulic fracturing operations in the absence of the final rule. The cost estimates in the RIA were developed after consulting the available literature and conferring with BLM's petroleum engineers and other knowledgeable professionals, and after considering the public comments on economic impacts and costs that were submitted as part of the rulemaking process, including those comments that were submitted to the Office of Management and Budget.

Based on that information, the RIA concluded that the rule will increase costs an average of $11,400 per hydraulically fractured well, or between 0.13 percent and 0.21 percent of the total cost of drilling and fracturing a typical oil and gas well. In those cases where fluid volumes exceed a certain threshold, we estimate that the compliance with the storage tank requirement could cost an operator $74,400 (representing approximately 0.8 to 1.4 percent of the cost of drilling a well). Through our analysis we estimate that this is only a small subset of total operations. These operations are those where the volumes of recovered fluids are expected to be very high and typically occur in states (Arkansas, Louisiana, Mississippi, Ohio, Oklahoma, and Pennsylvania) which represent only about 0.8% of estimated hydraulic fracturing activities on Federal and Indian land.

Given that the RIA estimates such a small relative increase in costs, we do not believe the rule will have a notable impact on oil and gas production from Federal lands. Business decisions like when and where to drill or hydraulically fracture a well are primarily driven by market factors and resource considerations, including commodity prices, geology, location relative to demand centers, availability of transportation infrastructure, and other critical factors. For example, in the Fort Berthold Indian Reservation, where the BLM serves as the permitting agency, oil production soared more than five-fold between 2008 and 2014--a faster increase than occurred on private lands. Overall, natural gas production on Federal and tribal lands in North Dakota is up over 200 percent, consistent with the statewide trend over that same period. These increases are due to the location of the Bakken shale and the favorable economics associated with developing that resource. In contrast, over the same period, some of the rural western fields where most of the Federal onshore production is located, are no longer economic under current prices because of their location relative to existing markets. The BLM has seen a decrease in production from those fields, tracking trends on state and private lands.

Question 2: BLM has not issued a final environmental impact statement (EIS) for an oil and gas production project in Wyoming since 2008. Currently, there are nine EISs for oil and gas production projects in Wyoming pending with BLM. Some of the EISs have been pending with BLM for more than 8 years. During the hearing, you said that "about half of those [project proposals] came in in the last two years." Of these nine, you indicated that BLM would issue two to three final EISs in Wyoming this year.

   A. **Would you please provide the date that each of the nine projects were first proposed to BLM?**

   B. **Would you please provide the date (month/year) when we can expect BLM to issue the final EIS for each of the nine projects?**

Response:

Currently, there are eight oil and gas Environmental Impact Statements (EISs) being prepared by BLM Wyoming, which are listed below. The LaBarge Platform Development Project EIS, included as one of the nine EISs previously referenced, was recently withdrawn by project proponents, who cited the inability to meet general conformity requirements for ozone.

All of the projects listed below are large in scope and scale, each involving thousands of wells. This scale makes the analysis of these projects complex and sensitive to oil and gas prices, which have been cited by project proponents as a factor in their requests for delays in processing. This scale also means that air quality standards and the associated modeling and mitigation efforts are a critical component of the review process. For example, some of the projects are located in areas that are in non-attainment for ozone, which requires additional analysis under the Clean Air Act. Another factor affecting review timelines is applicant-initiated changes in the plans of development (PODs) for the projects. These requested changes to PODs can require the BLM to restart the NEPA process because the proposed changes significantly alter the impact analysis. In the last two years, three PODs for these projects (Black Forest, Hiawatha, and Bird Canyon) have received substantial revisions, which have impacted timelines.

I also wish to take the opportunity to clarify my statement at the hearing. Upon further review, I did not have completely accurate information about these projects at the hearing. While the BLM received initial applications for most of the projects a number of years ago, several of the projects have undergone significant changes, which effectively required BLM to initiate analytical processes anew. I also should have said we are on track to issue two to three draft or final EISs in the coming year.

1. **Continental Divide – Creston Natural Gas Project EIS (Rawlins Field Office)**
   a. The Notice of Intent (NOI) to prepare an EIS was published in March 2006.
   b. Following publication of the NOI the POD underwent a number of significant revisions that increased the size of the project.
      - Air quality modeling was completed collaboratively with the Wyoming Department of Environmental Quality in January 2012.
   c. The Draft Environmental Impact Statement (DEIS) was released in December 2012.
   d. Comments received on the DEIS raised serious questions about the adequacy of the existing air quality modeling. As a result, an additional Air Quality Technical Support Document for the project was completed in 2014.
   e. Publication of the Final Environmental Impact Statement (FEIS) is anticipated for late 2015. Prior to finalization of the FEIS, the BLM has to confirm that the project is consistent with the recently approved land use plans for the Greater Sage Grouse, and that it complies with the Environmental Protection Agency's recently revised ozone standard.

2. **Black Fork EIS (Formerly Moxa Arch Area Infill) (Kemmerer Field Office)**
   a. The NOI to prepare an EIS was published in October 2005.
      - The Draft EIS was released in October 2007.
      - Anadarko Petroleum Corporation took over the project in December 2013, which resulted in the project being renamed. Anadarko also developed and submitted a new Plan of Development (POD) for the project in October 2014. The POD is still undergoing refinement based on discussions between the proponent and the BLM.
   b. Once the revisions to the new POD are complete, a new NOI will be issued and a project schedule will be developed.

3. **Hiawatha Field Project EIS (Rock Springs Field Office)**
   a. The NOI to prepare an EIS was published in September 2006.
   b. A DEIS was made available for administrative and Cooperating Agency review in 2007. This review identified concerns with the air emissions

inventory used for the air quality modeling. These concerns resulted in the Project's air quality analysis protocol being revised to make it consistent with the one use for the Black Fork Project (formerly Moxa Arch).

    c. In late-2014, the proponent revised the POD, which required the BLM to revisit the analysis in the administrative draft EIS and restructure some of the alternatives being analyzed. That work is in process.

    d. The DEIS is anticipated to be published in mid-2016.

4. **Normally-Pressured Lance Natural Gas Development Project EIS (Pinedale Field Office)**

    a. The NOI to prepare an EIS was published in April 2011.

    b. The applicant submitted a revised POD to BLM in June 2011.

    c. Because the project is located in a non-attainment area, air quality general conformity requirements must be completed before the DEIS can be finalized. Those efforts are in process and are anticipated to be completed soon, at which point the BLM will be in a position to develop a schedule for completion of the DEIS.

5. **Moneta Divide Natural Gas and Oil Development Project EIS (formerly GMI) (Lander Field Office)**

    a. An NOI was published in 2008.

    b. Following publication of the NOI, the applicant made substantial revisions to the POD--changes that resulted in, among other things, the inclusion of adjacent lands.

    c. Due to the size and magnitude of the revised project, the proposal was determined to require additional public notice and scoping.

    d. The NOI for the new proposal was published in January 2013.

    e. The DEIS is anticipated to be published in early 2016.

6. **Bird Canyon Field Infill Project EIS (Rock Springs Field Office)**

    a. The NOI to prepare an EIS was published May 2014.

    b. The DEIS is anticipated to be published late-2015.

7. **Converse County Oil and Gas Project EIS**: Casper Field Office

    a. The NOI to prepare an EIS was published in May 2014 and a POD was submitted in August 2014.

    b. The DEIS is anticipated to be published in mid-2016.

8. **Greater Crossbow Oil and Gas Project EIS**: Buffalo Field Office

    a. A POD was submitted to BLM in June 2014.

    b. The NOI is currently under review and is anticipated to be published in late 2015.

Question 3: On April 17, 2015, the Secretary of the Interior issued an advanced notice of proposed rulemaking for the purpose of seeking public comment on

potential updates to BLM rules governing oil and gas royalty rates, rental payments, lease sale minimum bids, civil penalty caps and financial assurances.

I am concerned that any proposal to raise royalty rates and other fees will put federal lands at an even greater competitive disadvantage with state and private lands—and, as a consequence, Wyoming and other public land states at a greater disadvantage with other areas of the country.
In 2011, DOI commissioned a study which found that higher royalty rates for federal lands in Wyoming "will deteriorate their competitive position in the market, which is rather weak as it is."

On March 14, 2012, then BLM Director, Bob Abbey, testified before the Senate that there has been "a shift [in oil and gas production] to private lands in the East and to the South where there are fewer amounts of Federal mineral estate."

According to the Energy Information Administration (EIA), federal onshore natural gas production has decreased by 22 percent since 2009. EIA has found that federal onshore natural gas production makes up a smaller percentage of total U.S. gas production than it has in at least 11 years. EIA has also found that federal onshore oil production makes up a smaller percentage of total U.S. oil production than it has in nine years. While these numbers reflect new production on state and private lands, they also show that federal lands are becoming less competitive with state and private lands.

Please explain, in detail, how raising the royalty rates on onshore oil and gas production on federal lands will not further reduce their competitive position relative to state and private lands. In your answer, please address the additional regulatory burdens, including those associated with the National Environmental Policy Act, which apply to oil and gas production on federal lands but not oil and gas production on state and private lands.

Response:

On April 21, 2015, the BLM published an Advanced Notice of Proposed Rulemaking (ANPR) to seek public comment on potential updates to BLM rules governing oil and gas royalty rates, rental payments, lease sale minimum bids, civil penalty caps and financial assurances. With regard to royalty rates, the ANPR sought comment on potential changes that would provide the BLM with the procedural flexibility to change the royalty rate in response to market conditions, similar to procedures currently in place for offshore oil and gas leases. The BLM extended the comment period to June 19, 2015, and received a total of over 82,000 comments, which are still under agency review.

Currently, the royalty rate for competitive oil and gas leases on public lands is fixed at 12.5 percent. As explained in the ANPR, many states and private landowners assess higher rates to oil and gas developed from their lands. With respect to the State of Wyoming, the State specifies a higher royalty rate on production from State lands than the BLM does for Federal lands for competitively issued parcels – 16.6 percent for State parcels obtained as part of competitive leases sales versus 12.5 percent for Federal parcels. Both Wyoming and the BLM charge a royalty rate of 12.5 percent for parcels that are obtained non-competitively. Any increase in the royalty rate assigned to Federal leases could increase revenue to the U.S. Treasury, as well as revenue to the individual states, given that the Federal Government shares royalty revenues with its state partners. In the lower 48 states, that revenue sharing is roughly a 50/50 split. Higher royalty rates could also have the effect of reducing the relative competitiveness of federal oil and gas leases, which could reduce the amount of oil and gas development and ultimately revenue. Before raising rates, BLM would carefully consider the impact on oil and gas development and seek input from the public including affected entities.

Evaluating whether an increase in royalty rate is appropriate is consistent with the BLM's obligation to ensure that the public receives a fair return on its resources while balancing economic, environmental, and other considerations, including requirements under the National Environmental Policy Act and other statutes. For example, the Federal Land Policy and Management Act of 1976 (FLPMA) directs the BLM to manage the public lands using the principles of multiple use and sustained yield and to take any action necessary to prevent unnecessary or undue degradation—an obligation that does not exist for state and private lands.

Potential changes to BLM's regulations would also respond to concerns expressed by the Government Accountability Office (GAO) and Interior's Office of Inspector General that the BLM's existing rules lack flexibility and could be causing the United States to forego significant revenue to the detriment of taxpayers.

With respect to the competitive position of Federal lands relative to state and private lands; as explained above, oil and gas investment decisions are principally driven by market factors and resource considerations, including commodity prices, geology, location relative to demand centers, and availability of transportation infrastructure, among many considerations. This is why, generally speaking, production trends on BLM-managed public lands have tracked broader state-wide trends despite the current difference in royalty rates applicable to Federal versus state and private minerals.

Question 4: I understand there are significant delays in obtaining sundry notices and rights-of-way (ROWs) for natural gas gathering lines on federal lands from BLM.

In February 2015, I asked Secretary Jewell to provide detailed information about pending requests for sundry notices and ROWs for natural gas gathering lines on federal land.

In response, the Secretary explained that BLM "lacks capability to query for details of each sundry notice" and BLM, with respect to requests for ROWs, "does not distinguish between requests for oil or gas, gathering or transport, lines."

A. What is the total number of requests for ROWs pending at BLM?

As of August 7, 2015, the total number of right-of-way (ROW) applications pending with the BLM is 867.

B. What is the total number of requests for ROWs pending at each BLM Field Office?

The table below shows the number of pending ROWs at each BLM field office. The data was collected from the BLM's bureau-wide digital land records system, LR2000, and is current as of August 7, 2015.

BLM PENDING O&G ROW PIPELINE APPLICATIONS (LR2000)	
BLM Field Office	**Pending Pipeline Applications**
AZ Total	**6**
Kingman Field Office	3
Safford Field Office	1
Yuma Field Office	2
CA Total	**69**
Bakersfield Field Office	65
Barstow Field Office	2
Needles Field Office	1
PalmSprings/S.Coast Field Office	1
CO Total	**33**
Colorado River Valley Field Office	10
Grand Junction Field Office	3
Little Snake Field Office	1
Northwest District Office	1
Royal Gorge Field Office	2
Tres Rios Field Office	3
White River Field Office	13
ES Total	**3**
Milwaukee Field Office	3
ID Total	**1**
Jarbidge Field Office	1
MT Total	**12**
Havre Field Office	2
Miles City Field Office	4
North Dakota Field Office	4
South Dakota Field Office	2
NM Total	**587**
Carlsbad Field Office	275
State Office*	1

BLM PENDING O&G ROW PIPELINE APPLICATIONS (LR2000)	
BLM Field Office	**Pending Pipeline Applications**
Farmington Field Office	300
Las Cruces District Office	2
Roswell Field Office	7
Taos Field Office	2

NV Total	**15**
State Office*	7
Las Vegas Field Office	2
Sierra Front Field Office	2
Stillwater Field Office	1
Tuscarora Field Office	1
Winnemucca District Office	1
Winnemucca Field Office	1
OR Total	**2**
Prineville Deschutes Field Office	1
Spokane Wenatchee Field Office	1
UT Total	**28**
Fillmore Field Office	1
Moab Field Office	2
Monticello Field Office	1
Price Field Office	2
Richfield Field Office	2
Vernal Field Office	20
WY Total	**111**
Casper Field Office	11
Cody Field Office	1
Kemmerer Field Office	8
Lander Field Office	1
Newcastle Field Office	2
Pinedale Field Office	29
Rawlins Field Office	31
Rock Springs Field Office	26
Worland Field Office	2
BLM Total	**867**

*Note: Applications pending in a state office.

C. When were each of the pending requests for ROWs first submitted to BLM?

The table below shows the date each pending ROW was submitted to a BLM field office. The data was collected from the BLM's bureau-wide digital land records system, LR2000, and is current as of August 7, 2015, to the extent such information is available. It should be noted that information is manually entered into the LR2000, and therefore there is always the potential for data entry errors.

State and Field Office	Serial Number	Date Received
ARIZONA		
Kingman Field Office	AZA 035936	05/06/2011
	AZA 036782	05/18/2015
	AZA 036783	05/18/2015
Kingman Field Office Total	**3**	
Safford Field Office	AZA 032511	07/29/2003
Safford Field Office Total	**1**	
Yuma Field Office	AZA 033088	03/24/2005
	AZA 035790	09/27/2011
Yuma Field Office Total	**2**	
AZ TOTAL	**6**	
CALIFORNIA		
Bakersfield Field Office	CACA 015634A	02/10/2010
	CACA 030806A	02/19/2010
	CACA 051668	02/19/2010
	CACA 051669	02/19/2010
	CACA 051670	02/19/2010
	CACA 051678	02/25/2010
	CAS 0033318A	02/25/2010
	CACA 051690	03/04/2010
	CACA 051691	03/04/2010
	CACA 051692	03/04/2010
	CACA 051693	03/04/2010
	CACA 051694	03/04/2010
	CACA 051695	03/04/2010
	CACA 051815	04/16/2010
	CACA 051816	04/16/2010
	CACA 051818	04/16/2010
	CACA 051819	04/16/2010
	CACA 051820	04/16/2010
	CACA 051822	04/16/2010
	CACA 051823	04/16/2010
	CACA 051834	04/20/2010
	CACA 051900	04/30/2010
	CACA 051901	04/30/2010
	CACA 051902	04/30/2010
	CACA 051903	04/30/2010
	CACA 051904	04/30/2010
	CACA 051906	04/30/2010
	CACA 051907	04/30/2010
	CACA 051908	04/30/2010
	CACA 051909	04/30/2010
	CACA 051910	04/30/2010

State and Field Office	Serial Number	Date Received
	CACA 051911	04/30/2010
	CACA 051912	04/30/2010
	CACA 051913	04/30/2010
	CACA 051914	04/30/2010
	CACA 051915	04/30/2010
	CACA 051916	04/30/2010
	CACA 051917	04/30/2010
	CACA 051918	04/30/2010
	CACA 051919	04/30/2010
	CACA 051920	04/30/2010
	CACA 051921	04/30/2010
	CACA 051922	04/30/2010
	CACA 051923	04/30/2010
	CACA 051924	04/30/2010
	CACA 051925	04/30/2010
	CACA 051926	04/30/2010
	CACA 051927	04/30/2010
	CACA 051928	04/30/2010
	CACA 051929	04/30/2010
	CACA 051930	04/30/2010
	CACA 051931	04/30/2010
	CACA 051932	04/30/2010
	CACA 051933	04/30/2010
	CACA 051934	04/30/2010
	CACA 051935	04/30/2010
	CACA 051936	04/30/2010
	CACA 051937	04/30/2010
	CACA 051938	04/30/2010
	CACA 051939	04/30/2010
	CACA 051940	04/30/2010
	CACA 051941	04/30/2010
	CACA 051942	04/30/2010
	CACA 051989	04/30/2010
	CACA 054624	05/14/2013
Bakersfield Field Office Total	**65**	
Barstow Field Office	CACA 049138	06/18/2007
	CACA 054469	03/12/2013
Barstow Field Office Total	**2**	
Needles Field Office	CACA 053550	01/31/2012
Needles Field Office Total	**1**	

Palm Springs/S Coast Field Office	CACA 051203	07/15/2009
Palm Springs/S Coast Field Office Total	**1**	
CA TOTAL	**69**	
COLORADO		
Colorado River Valley Field Office	COC 071059	04/10/2007
	COC 076335	04/18/2013
	COC 076339	09/23/2013
	COC 076339T	09/23/2013
	COC 076552	02/05/2014
	COC 076553	02/05/2014
	COC 076833	11/06/2014
	COC 077059	02/05/2015
	COC 077107	03/24/2015
	COC 077155	04/29/2015
Colorado River Valley Field Office Total	**10**	
Grand Junction Field Office	COC 074659	09/21/2010
	COC 03517501	02/15/2011
	COC 077238	10/23/2014
Grand Junction Field Office Total	**3**	
Little Snake Field Office	COC 076721	09/22/2014
Little Snake Field Office Total	**1**	
Northwest District Office	COC 076044	02/06/2013
Northwest District Office Total	**1**	
Royal Gorge Field Office	COC 076865	10/27/2014
	COC 076866	10/27/2014
Royal Gorge Field Office Total	**2**	
Tres Rios Field Office	COC 068759	05/16/2005
	COC 069363	07/13/2005
	COC 070301	06/10/2006
Tres Rios Field Office Total	**3**	

White River Field Office	COC 077227	11/30/2006
	COC 074630	08/12/2009
	COC 074470	04/12/2010
	COC 074753	04/12/2010
	COC 076298	04/24/2012
	COC 075627	08/24/2012
	COC 076577	05/07/2014
	COC 076583	06/02/2014
	COC 077001	08/06/2014
	COC 076768	08/20/2014
	COC 077167	10/31/2014
	COC 077078	12/09/2014
	COC 077136	03/02/2015
White River Field Office Total	**13**	
CO TOTAL	**33**	
EASTERN STATES		
Milwaukee Field Office	ILES 057973	10/28/2013
	VAES 058078	01/26/2015
	WVES 058077	01/26/2015
Milwaukee Field Office Total	**3**	
ES TOTAL	**3**	
IDAHO		
Jarbidge Field Office	IDI 037927	03/05/2015
Jarbidge Field Office Total	**1**	
ID TOTAL	**1**	
MONTANA/DAKOTAS		
Havre Field Office	MTM 108271	05/04/2015
	MTM 108269	06/01/2015
Havre Field Office Total	**2**	
Miles City Field Office	MTM 098191	03/20/2008
	MTM 098482	08/05/2008
	MTM 098695	10/20/2008
	MTM 103484	07/06/2011
Miles City Field Office Total	**4**	
North Dakota Field Office	NDM 107833	09/05/2014
	NDM 107834	09/05/2014
	NDM 107871	10/06/2014
	NDM 108240	05/11/2015
North Dakota Field Office Total	**5**	
South Dakota Field Office	SDM 099292	06/18/2009
	SDM 107311	01/02/2014
South Dakota Field Office Total	**2**	
MT TOTAL	**12**	

NEW MEXICO		
Carlsbad Field Office	NMNM 0070225A	08/10/1959
	NMLM 084516	10/24/2002
	NMLM 109818	05/08/2003
	NMLM 110720	09/15/2003
	NMNM 011312	04/21/2004
	NMNM 130171	06/01/2004
	NMNM 113327	06/20/2005
	NMNM 117709	01/27/2007
	NMNM 117847	02/14/2007
	NMNM 118415	05/15/2007
	NMNM 120726	05/29/2008
	NMNM 121687	11/17/2008
	NMNM 122236	02/26/2009
	NMNM 123454	07/08/2009
	NMNM 124583	11/16/2009
	NMNM 124183	12/10/2009
	NMNM 124691	03/19/2010
	NMNM 124038A	05/18/2010
	NMNM 12477401	07/06/2010
	NMNM 125478	09/03/2010
	NMNM 125523	09/20/2010
	NMNM 126328	03/08/2011
	NMNM 126477	04/12/2011
	NMNM 126589	05/05/2011
	NMNM 126836	05/10/2011
	NMNM 126693	05/17/2011
	NMNM 126884	07/06/2011
	NMNM 127334	09/14/2011
	NMNM 127735	10/13/2011
	NMNM 127977	01/17/2012
	NMNM 12562401	01/23/2012
	NMNM 127954	01/24/2012
	NMNM 128732	06/18/2012
	NMNM 128761	07/02/2012
	NMNM 128932	08/07/2012
	NMNM 128823	10/04/2012
	NMNM 129454	11/14/2012
	NMNM 129896	01/07/2013
	NMNM 129931	01/29/2013
	NMNM 130301	04/15/2013
	NMNM 131086	06/06/2013
	NMNM 131505	06/11/2013
	NMNM 130735	06/13/2013
	NMNM 131561	07/29/2013

	NMNM	131144	07/31/2013
	NMNM	131295	08/20/2013
	NMNM	131292	09/12/2013
	NMNM	131390	09/24/2013
	NMNM	131400	10/21/2013
	NMNM	131499	10/31/2013
	NMNM	131610	11/12/2013
	NMNM	131612	11/12/2013
	NMNM	132002	11/25/2013
	NMNM	131822	12/05/2013
	NMNM	131803	12/13/2013
	NMNM	131763	12/17/2013
	NMNM	131841	12/30/2013
	NMNM	131820	01/07/2014
	NMNM	131834	01/08/2014
	NMNM	132174	02/20/2014
	NMNM	132196	02/20/2014
	NMNM	132252	02/26/2014
	NMNM	132301	03/10/2014
	NMNM	094320A	03/12/2014
	NMNM	132302	03/13/2014
	NMNM	132376	03/23/2014
	NMNM	132375	03/25/2014
	NMNM	132491	04/04/2014
	NMNM	132556	04/17/2014
	NMNM	132644	04/17/2014
	NMNM	132606	04/21/2014
	NMNM	132607	04/21/2014
	NMNM	132654	04/23/2014
	NMNM	132596	04/24/2014
	NMNM	132603	04/24/2014
	NMNM	132605	04/24/2014
	NMNM	132551	04/25/2014
	NMNM	132667	04/29/2014
	NMNM	132585	04/30/2014
	NMNM	132694	05/05/2014
	NMNM	132718	05/05/2014
	NMNM	132534	05/07/2014
	NMNM	132919	05/27/2014
	NMNM	132697	05/29/2014
	NMNM	132775	05/29/2014
	NMNM	132711	06/06/2014
	NMNM	132901	06/09/2014
	NMNM	132777	06/12/2014
	NMNM	133288	06/23/2014

NMNM	132961	06/30/2014
NMNM	133111	06/30/2014
NMNM	133224	07/03/2014
NMNM	133108	07/15/2014
NMNM	133085	07/16/2014
NMNM	133136	07/21/2014
NMNM	133708	07/21/2014
NMNM	133205	07/23/2014
NMNM	133088	07/28/2014
NMNM	133093	07/28/2014
NMNM	133143	07/28/2014
NMNM	133144	07/28/2014
NMNM	133771	07/29/2014
NMNM	133770	08/04/2014
NMNM	133199	08/07/2014
NMNM	133207	08/07/2014
NMNM	133216	08/07/2014
NMNM	133308	08/12/2014
NMNM	133282	08/19/2014
NMNM	133171	08/22/2014
NMNM	133654	09/03/2014
NMNM	133671	09/03/2014
NMNM	133366	09/09/2014
NMNM	133651	09/09/2014
NMNM	133360	09/12/2014
NMNM	133462	09/13/2014
NMNM	133313	09/15/2014
NMNM	133386	09/15/2014
NMNM	133387	09/15/2014
NMNM	133582	09/18/2014
NMNM	133385	09/24/2014
NMNM	133707	09/25/2014
NMNM	133737	09/25/2014
NMNM	133836	09/25/2014
NMNM	133435	09/29/2014
NMNM	133580	09/29/2014
NMNM	133523	10/07/2014
NMNM	133780	10/07/2014
NMNM	133822	10/09/2014
NMNM	133527	10/14/2014
NMNM	133601	10/15/2014
NMNM	133637	10/15/2014
NMNM	134103	10/15/2014
NMNM	133641	10/20/2014
NMNM	133653	10/20/2014

	NMNM 133792	10/20/2014
	NMNM 134062	10/22/2014
	NMNM 134167	10/22/2014
	NMNM 133696	10/24/2014
	NMNM 134006	10/27/2014
	NMNM 133657	10/28/2014
	NMNM 133788	10/28/2014
	NMNM 133789	10/28/2014
	NMNM 133944	10/28/2014
	NMNM 133947	10/28/2014
	NMNM 134260	10/28/2014
	NMNM 133629	10/30/2014
	NMNM 133632	10/30/2014
	NMNM 133633	10/30/2014
	NMNM 133643	11/03/2014
	NMNM 133662	11/03/2014
	NMNM 133666	11/03/2014
	NMNM 134061	11/03/2014
	NMNM 133675	11/04/2014
	NMNM 133640	11/06/2014
	NMNM 133684	11/10/2014
	NMNM 133628	11/13/2014
	NMNM 134090	11/14/2014
	NMNM 133718	11/17/2014
	NMNM 134198	11/17/2014
	NMNM 133626	11/18/2014
	NMNM 133791	11/23/2014
	NMNM 133794	11/25/2014
	NMNM 134299	11/25/2014
	NMNM 133786	12/01/2014
	NMNM 133787	12/01/2014
	NMNM 133739	12/02/2014
	NMNM 133746	12/02/2014
	NMNM 133817	12/02/2014
	NMNM 134101	12/05/2014
	NMNM 133880	12/08/2014
	NMNM 133882	12/10/2014
	NMNM 134266	12/12/2014
	NMNM 133863	12/15/2014
	NMNM 133876	12/16/2014
	NMNM 133883	12/17/2014
	NMNM 133998	12/24/2014
	NMNM 133936	01/06/2015
	NMNM 134082	01/07/2015
	NMNM 133120	01/08/2015

	NMNM 133931	01/08/2015
	NMNM 133018	01/12/2015
	NMNM 133917	01/12/2015
	NMNM 133953	01/12/2015
	NMNM 134009	01/12/2015
	NMNM 134024	01/12/2015
	NMNM 134025	01/12/2015
	NMNM 134007	01/13/2015
	NMNM 134255	01/14/2015
	NMNM 134023	01/22/2015
	NMNM 133973	01/26/2015
	NMNM 134067	01/27/2015
	NMNM 134069	01/27/2015
	NMNM 134070	01/27/2015
	NMNM 134115	01/27/2015
	NMNM 134015	01/29/2015
	NMNM 134119	02/03/2015
	NMNM 134193	02/03/2015
	NMNM 134091	02/04/2015
	NMNM 134114	02/09/2015
	NMNM 134145	02/19/2015
	NMNM 134139	02/20/2015
	NMNM 134150	02/20/2015
	NMNM 134194	02/23/2015
	NMNM 134200	02/24/2015
	NMNM 134256	03/04/2015
	NMNM 134244	03/10/2015
	NMNM 134261	03/10/2015
	NMNM 134437	03/10/2015
	NMNM 133634	03/12/2015
	NMNM 134300	03/20/2015
	NMNM 134307	03/23/2015
	NMNM 134311	03/24/2015
	NMNM 134337	03/24/2015
	NMNM 134339	03/26/2015
	NMNM 134369	03/30/2015
	NMNM 134357	04/01/2015
	NMNM 134366	04/02/2015
	NMNM 134377	04/08/2015
	NMNM 134382	04/09/2015
	NMNM 134396	04/13/2015
	NMNM 134399	04/14/2015
	NMNM 134412	04/16/2015
	NMNM 134413	04/16/2015
	NMNM 134414	04/16/2015

	NMNM 134415	04/16/2015
	NMNM 134416	04/16/2015
	NMNM 134418	04/16/2015
	NMNM 134421	04/16/2015
	NMNM 134422	04/16/2015
	NMNM 134423	04/17/2015
	NMNM 134428	04/21/2015
	NMNM 134459	04/24/2015
	NMNM 134499	05/08/2015
	NMNM 134500	05/08/2015
	NMNM 134503	05/08/2015
	NMNM 134524	05/13/2015
	NMNM 134526	05/13/2015
	NMNM 134548	05/19/2015
	NMNM 134550	05/19/2015
	NMNM 134561	05/20/2015
	NMNM 134597	05/22/2015
	NMNM 134606	06/01/2015
	NMNM 134624	06/04/2015
	NMNM 134630	06/08/2015
	NMNM 134632	06/08/2015
	NMNM 134634	06/08/2015
	NMNM 134636	06/08/2015
	NMNM 134637	06/08/2015
	NMNM 134647	06/11/2015
	NMNM 134648	06/11/2015
	NMNM 134658	06/15/2015
	NMNM 134662	06/17/2015
	NMNM 134663	06/17/2015
	NMNM 134667	06/17/2015
	NMNM 134668	06/17/2015
	NMNM 134669	06/17/2015
	NMNM 134670	06/17/2015
	NMNM 134678	06/19/2015
	NMNM 134688	06/22/2015
	NMNM 134690	06/22/2015
	NMNM 134691	06/22/2015
	NMNM 134701	06/24/2015
	NMNM 134725	06/29/2015
	NMNM 134726	06/30/2015
	NMNM 134748	07/06/2015
	NMNM 134750	07/06/2015
	NMNM 134751	07/06/2015
	NMNM 134794	07/06/2015
	NMNM 134795	07/06/2015

	NMNM 134797	07/08/2015
	NMNM 134790	07/10/2015
	NMNM 134845	07/20/2015
	NMNM 134922	07/22/2015
	NMNM 134930	07/24/2015
	NMNM 134945	07/30/2015
Carlsbad Field Office Total	**275**	
New Mexico State Office	NMNM 128389	04/18/2012
New Mexico State Office Total	**1**	
Farmington Field Office	NMNM 088300	06/22/1992
	NMNM 095124	06/30/1995
	NMNM 101936	01/14/1999
	NMNM 107825	04/11/2002
	NMNM 109525	02/06/2003
	NMNM 110038	07/31/2003
	NMNM 111572	02/19/2004
	NMNM 113740	05/26/2005
	NMNM 113807	07/18/2005
	NMNM 114844	09/22/2005
	NMNM 114885	09/26/2005
	NMNM 114918	10/04/2005
	NMNM 115060	10/18/2005
	NMNM 115078	10/20/2005
	NMNM 115482	01/20/2006
	NMNM 115673	02/15/2006
	NMNM 115681	02/15/2006
	NMNM 115902	03/24/2006
	NMNM 115931	03/30/2006
	NMNM 115950	04/03/2006
	NMNM 116140	04/27/2006
	NMNM 116193	04/28/2006
	NMNM 116217	05/01/2006
	NMNM 116221	05/01/2006
	NMNM 116222	05/01/2006
	NMNM 116974	05/26/2006
	NMNM 116478	06/27/2006
	NMNM 116499	07/06/2006
	NMNM 116637	07/19/2006
	NMNM 116640	07/19/2006
	NMNM 116642	07/19/2006
	NMNM 116697	07/28/2006
	NMNM 116867	08/28/2006
	NMNM 116849	08/29/2006
	NMNM 116894	09/06/2006

	NMNM	116963	09/21/2006
	NMNM	117301	11/15/2006
	NMNM	117392	12/01/2006
	NMNM	117448	12/15/2006
	NMNM	117449	12/15/2006
	NMNM	117754	02/07/2007
	NMNM	117787	02/12/2007
	NMNM	117790	02/12/2007
	NMNM	117889	03/02/2007
	NMNM	118069	04/04/2007
	NMNM	118306	05/02/2007
	NMNM	118307	05/02/2007
	NMNM	118331	05/09/2007
	NMNM	118339	05/11/2007
	NMNM	118498	06/18/2007
	NMNM	118597	07/09/2007
	NMNM	118598	07/09/2007
	NMNM	118651	07/16/2007
	NMNM	118989	07/26/2007
	NMNM	118878	07/27/2007
	NMNM	118948	08/03/2007
	NMNM	119171	09/19/2007
	NMNM	119194	09/25/2007
	NMNM	118932	09/28/2007
	NMNM	119427	11/05/2007
	NMNM	119431	11/05/2007
	NMNM	11946001	11/13/2007
	NMNM	119508	11/28/2007
	NMNM	119509	11/28/2007
	NMNM	119535	12/03/2007
	NMNM	119880	01/23/2008
	NMNM	119882	01/23/2008
	NMNM	119886	01/23/2008
	NMNM	119971	02/07/2008
	NMNM	119973	02/07/2008
	NMNM	119977	02/07/2008
	NMNM	120004	02/12/2008
	NMNM	12006801	02/25/2008
	NMNM	120087	03/03/2008
	NMNM	120238	03/24/2008
	NMNM	120249	03/31/2008
	NMNM	120289	04/07/2008
	NMNM	120428	04/21/2008
	NMNM	120429	04/21/2008
	NMNM	120546	04/30/2008

	NMNM 120573	05/07/2008
	NMNM 120601	05/13/2008
	NMNM 120599	05/14/2008
	NMNM 120989	07/16/2008
	NMNM 121217	08/04/2008
	NMNM 121208	08/26/2008
	NMNM 121214	08/26/2008
	NMNM 121589	10/23/2008
	NMNM 122018	01/27/2009
	NMNM 122083	01/30/2009
	NMNM 122092	02/05/2009
	NMNM 122121	02/06/2009
	NMNM 122122	02/06/2009
	NMNM 122125	02/06/2009
	NMNM 122126	02/06/2009
	NMNM 117775	02/08/2009
	NMNM 122130	02/09/2009
	NMNM 122131	02/09/2009
	NMNM 122132	02/09/2009
	NMNM 122107	02/11/2009
	NMNM 122164	02/17/2009
	NMNM 122167	02/17/2009
	NMNM 122170	02/20/2009
	NMNM 122288	03/17/2009
	NMNM 122331	03/20/2009
	NMNM 122333	03/20/2009
	NMNM 122334	03/20/2009
	NMNM 122335	03/20/2009
	NMNM 122429	04/08/2009
	NMNM 123103	04/30/2009
	NMNM 123226	05/11/2009
	NMNM 123248	05/15/2009
	NMNM 123242	05/19/2009
	NMNM 123354	06/11/2009
	NMNM 123985	09/29/2009
	NMNM 124048	09/30/2009
	NMNM 124049	09/30/2009
	NMNM 124176	12/30/2009
	NMNM 124359	02/10/2010
	NMNM 126150	05/04/2010
	NMNM 124971	06/03/2010
	NMNM 125042	06/23/2010
	NMNM 125046	06/28/2010
	NMNM 125121	07/08/2010
	NMNM 125302	07/21/2010

	NMNM	125342	08/02/2010
	NMNM	125447	08/30/2010
	NMNM	125681	10/18/2010
	NMNM	125816	11/05/2010
	NMNM	125892	12/02/2010
	NMNM	125894	12/02/2010
	NMNM	126021	01/06/2011
	NMNM	126022	01/06/2011
	NMNM	126023	01/06/2011
	NMNM	126263	02/24/2011
	NMNM	126536	04/14/2011
	NMNM	126539	04/14/2011
	NMNM	126540	04/14/2011
	NMNM	126542	04/14/2011
	NMNM	126531	04/21/2011
	NMNM	126753	06/03/2011
	NMNM	126745	06/07/2011
	NMNM	126748	06/07/2011
	NMNM	126858	06/23/2011
	NMNM	126867	06/30/2011
	NMNM	127013	07/20/2011
	NMNM	127021	07/20/2011
	NMNM	127182	08/20/2011
	NMNM	127320	09/15/2011
	NMNM	127321	09/15/2011
	NMNM	127363	09/29/2011
	NMNM	127500	10/25/2011
	NMNM	127583	11/09/2011
	NMNM	127584	11/09/2011
	NMNM	127588	11/09/2011
	NMNM	127622	11/18/2011
	NMNM	127780	11/22/2011
	NMNM	127982	01/10/2012
	NMNM	127983	01/10/2012
	NMNM	127990	01/27/2012
	NMNM	127991	01/27/2012
	NMNM	128037	02/02/2012
	NMNM	12803701	02/02/2012
	NMNM	12803901	02/02/2012
	NMNM	128168	03/01/2012
	NMNM	128538	05/04/2012
	NMNM	128780	06/28/2012
	NMNM	128968	08/09/2012
	NMNM	129055	08/29/2012
	NMNM	129207	09/12/2012

	NMNM 129206	09/14/2012
	NMNM 129204	09/21/2012
	NMNM 129202	10/03/2012
	NMNM 129345	10/15/2012
	NMNM 129635	10/31/2012
	NMNM 129643	11/05/2012
	NMNM 129646	11/05/2012
	NMNM 129644	11/09/2012
	NMNM 129651	11/09/2012
	NMNM 129652	11/09/2012
	NMNM 129676	11/28/2012
	NMNM 129666	12/12/2012
	NMNM 129856	01/02/2013
	NMNM 129865	01/09/2013
	NMNM 129874	01/14/2013
	NMNM 129877	01/15/2013
	NMNM 129925	02/05/2013
	NMNM 129926	02/05/2013
	NMNM 129964	02/12/2013
	NMNM 129966	02/12/2013
	NMNM 129977	02/13/2013
	NMNM 129981	02/13/2013
	NMNM 130019	02/19/2013
	NMNM 130037	02/22/2013
	NMNM 130110	03/05/2013
	NMNM 130163	03/13/2013
	NMNM 130164	03/13/2013
	NMNM 130201	03/21/2013
	NMNM 130467	04/24/2013
	NMNM 130468	04/24/2013
	NMNM 130470	05/01/2013
	NMNM 130685	06/13/2013
	NMNM 130819	07/08/2013
	NMNM 130917	07/15/2013
	NMNM 130937	07/19/2013
	NMNM 131289	09/05/2013
	NMNM 131694	12/03/2013
	NMNM 131954	01/23/2014
	NMNM 131935	01/24/2014
	NMNM 132010	02/12/2014
	NMNM 132014	02/12/2014
	NMNM 132017	02/12/2014
	NMNM 132020	02/12/2014
	NMNM 132188	03/03/2014
	NMNM 132190	03/05/2014

	NMNM 132231	03/10/2014
	NMNM 132232	03/10/2014
	NMNM 132233	03/10/2014
	NMNM 132370	04/04/2014
	NMNM 132433	04/04/2014
	NMNM 132440	04/04/2014
	NMNM 132447	04/04/2014
	NMNM 132571	05/15/2014
	NMNM 132600	05/22/2014
	NMNM 132730	05/22/2014
	NMNM 132680	06/02/2014
	NMNM 132685	06/02/2014
	NMNM 132765	06/04/2014
	NMNM 132735	06/17/2014
	NMNM 132827	06/30/2014
	NMNM 132842	06/30/2014
	NMNM 132868	06/30/2014
	NMNM 132874	06/30/2014
	NMNM 132875	06/30/2014
	NMNM 132885	06/30/2014
	NMNM 132886	06/30/2014
	NMNM 132881	07/03/2014
	NMNM 132967	07/16/2014
	NMNM 133049	07/28/2014
	NMNM 133050	07/28/2014
	NMNM 133052	07/31/2014
	NMNM 133055	07/31/2014
	NMNM 133097	07/31/2014
	NMNM 133101	08/06/2014
	NMNM 133220	08/20/2014
	NMNM 133223	08/21/2014
	NMNM 133233	08/21/2014
	NMNM 133249	08/21/2014
	NMNM 133252	08/21/2014
	NMNM 133328	09/11/2014
	NMNM 133410	09/29/2014
	NMNM 133411	09/29/2014
	NMNM 133412	09/29/2014
	NMNM 133413	09/29/2014
	NMNM 133415	09/29/2014
	NMNM 133417	09/30/2014
	NMNM 133420	10/02/2014
	NMNM 133433	10/02/2014
	NMNM 133554	10/03/2014
	NMNM 133540	10/10/2014

	NMNM 133515	10/15/2014
	NMNM 133519	10/15/2014
	NMNM 133796	12/12/2014
	NMNM 133825	12/19/2014
	NMNM 133888	01/06/2015
	NMNM 133893	01/06/2015
	NMNM 133895	01/07/2015
	NMNM 133897	01/07/2015
	NMNM 133905	01/08/2015
	NMNM 133906	01/08/2015
	NMNM 133915	01/08/2015
	NMNM 133987	01/16/2015
	NMNM 133974	01/20/2015
	NMNM 134207	02/03/2015
	NMNM 134217	02/19/2015
	NMNM 134220	02/19/2015
	NMNM 134223	02/19/2015
	NMNM 134276	03/05/2015
	NMNM 134282	03/05/2015
	NMNM 134287	03/05/2015
	NMNM 134290	03/05/2015
	NMNM 134306	03/16/2015
	NMNM 134308	03/16/2015
	NMNM 134304	03/19/2015
	NMNM 134305	03/19/2015
	NMNM 134309	03/23/2015
	NMNM 134371	03/25/2015
	NMNM 134346	03/27/2015
	NMNM 134454	04/07/2015
	NMNM 134467	04/10/2015
	NMNM 134451	04/13/2015
	NMNM 134577	04/21/2015
	NMNM 134578	05/13/2015
	NMNM 134582	05/13/2015
	NMNM 134596	05/26/2015
	NMNM 134685	06/08/2015
	NMNM 134695	06/11/2015
	NMNM 134765	06/29/2015
	NMNM 134719	07/02/2015
	NMNM 134955	07/27/2015
Farmington Field Office Total	**300**	
Las Cruces District Office	NMNM 131777	NMNM 131777
	NMNM 134401	NMNM 134401
Las Cruces District Office Total	**2**	

Roswell Field Office	NMNM 120114	03/10/2008
	NMNM 124445	02/26/2010
	NMNM 125090	07/07/2010
	NMNM 133609	11/14/2014
	NMNM 133615	11/14/2014
	NMNM 133926	01/15/2015
	NMNM 134758	07/06/2015
Roswell Field Office Total	**2**	
Taos Field Office	NMNM 128556	02/07/2012
	NMNM 133382	09/30/2014
Taos Field Office Total	**2**	
NM TOTAL	**587**	
NEVADA		
Nevada State Office	NVN 091207	05/31/2012
	NVN 093938	04/08/2015
	NVN 093979	04/30/2015
	NVN 09397901	04/30/2015
	NVN 093981	04/30/2015
	NVN 093983	04/30/2015
	NVN 093998	04/30/2015
State Office Total	**7**	
Las Vegas Field Office	NVN 048332	04/08/1988
	NVN 082066	05/23/2006
Las Vegas Field Office Total	**2**	
Sierra Front Field Office	NVN 084728	02/14/2008
	NVN 093884	03/05/2015
Sierra Front Field Office Total	**2**	
Stillwater Field Office	NVN 006344001	02/05/2014
Stillwater Field Office Total	**1**	
Tuscarora Field Office	NVN 092738	10/17/2013
Tuscarora Field Office Total	**1**	
Winnemucca District Office	NVN 094010	04/27/2015
Winnemucca District Office Total	**1**	
Winnemucca Field Office	NVN 084527	12/26/2007
Winnemucca Field Office Total	**1**	
NV TOTAL	**15**	
OREGON		
Prineville Deschutes Field Office	OROR 064443	06/26/2007
Prineville Deschutes Field	**1**	

Office Total		
Spokane Wenatchee Field Office	WAOR 052141	06/23/1995
Spokane Wenatchee Field Office Total	**1**	
OR TOTAL	**2**	
UTAH		
Fillmore Field Office	UTU 090095	09/06/2013
Fillmore Field Office Total	**1**	
Moab Field Office	UTU 088288	08/06/2010
	UTU 090680	07/22/2014
Moab Field Office Total	**2**	
Monticello Field Office	UTU 091275	06/15/2015
Monticello Field Office Total	**1**	
Price Field Office	UTU 091003	11/12/2014
	UTU 091010	11/24/2014
Price Field Office Total	**2**	
Richfield Field Office	UTU 090169	11/07/2013
	UTU 090255	01/09/2014
Richfield Field Office Total	**2**	
Vernal Field Office	UTU 087897	09/17/2009
	UTU 089094	05/18/2012
	UTU 089449	12/03/2012
	UTU 089452	12/03/2012
	UTU 090045	04/17/2013
	UTU 090063	07/16/2013
	UTU 090065	07/16/2013
	UTU 090068	07/16/2013
	UTU 090071	07/16/2013
	UTU 090073	07/16/2013
	UTU 090077	07/16/2013
	UTU 090831	07/16/2014
	UTU 090838	07/22/2014
	UTU 091164	01/16/2015
	UTU 091167	01/16/2015
	UTU 091235	02/04/2015
	UTU 091240	02/11/2015
	UTU 091279	06/25/2015
	UTU 091285	07/16/2015
	UTU 091286	07/16/2015
Vernal Field Office Total	**20**	
UT TOTAL	**28**	

WYOMING			
Casper Field Office	WYW	181474	07/02/1920
	WYW	118960	05/22/1990
	WYW	164156	07/21/2005
	WYW	181575	06/21/2007
	WYW	179847	09/29/2010
	WYW	180419	08/24/2011
	WYW	26653001	12/17/2012
	WYW	184326	03/10/2015
	WYW	184336	03/10/2015
	WYW	184338	03/10/2015
	WYW	184339	03/10/2015
Casper Field Office Total	**11**		
Cody Field Office	WYW	165784	05/08/2006
Cody Field Office Total	**1**		
Kemmerer Field Office	WYW	170987	10/20/2006
	WYW	170998	10/27/2006
	WYW	171067	04/05/2007
	WYW	171080	05/02/2007
	WYW	171148	10/29/2007
	WYW	171164	01/22/2008
	WYW	171285	10/13/2009
	WYW	171480	07/29/2015
Kemmerer Field Office Total	**8**		
Lander Field Office	WYW	168290	02/19/2013
Lander Field Office Total	**1**		
Newcastle Field Office	WYW	182443	07/26/2013
	WYW	170158	02/18/2015
Newcastle Field Office Total	**2**		
Pinedale Field Office	WYW	175307	10/08/2007
	WYW	175522	10/29/2008
	WYW	175537	11/14/2008
	WYW	175540	11/14/2008
	WYW	175541	11/24/2008
	WYW	175542	11/24/2008
	WYW	176916	03/30/2009
	WYW	176961	07/29/2009
	WYW	176963	08/06/2009
	WYW	176964	08/06/2009
	WYW	176965	08/11/2009
	WYW	176966	08/11/2009
	WYW	176967	08/11/2009
	WYW	176975	08/24/2009
	WYW	176976	08/24/2009
	WYW	181679	05/20/2014

	WYW	183494	03/31/2015
	WYW	183495	03/31/2015
	WYW	183497	03/31/2015
	WYW	183482	04/01/2015
	WYW	183503	06/22/2015
	WYW	183510	07/07/2015
	WYW	183511	07/16/2015
	WYW	183512	07/16/2015
	WYW	183513	07/16/2015
	WYW	183514	07/16/2015
	WYW	183518	07/30/2015
	WYW	183519	07/31/2015
	WYW	183520	07/31/2015
Pinedale Field Office Total	**29**		
Rawlins Field Office	WYW	166307	05/20/2009
	WYW	182426	07/18/2011
	WYW	183664	04/02/2012
	WYW	181254	06/27/2012
	WYW	181461	08/10/2012
	WYW	182667	09/18/2013
	WYW	182928	12/23/2013
	WYW	183857	03/27/2014
	WYW	183715	04/14/2014
	WYW	183716	04/14/2014
	WYW	183717	04/14/2014
	WYW	183718	04/14/2014
	WYW	183719	04/14/2014
	WYW	183727	06/24/2014
	WYW	183728	06/24/2014
	WYW	182665	09/16/2014
	WYW	184314	04/13/2015
	WYW	184321	04/15/2015
	WYW	184325	04/15/2015
	WYW	184333	04/24/2015
	WYW	184344	05/01/2015
	WYW	184431	05/12/2015
	WYW	184432	05/12/2015
	WYW	184451	05/26/2015
	WYW	184452	05/26/2015
	WYW	184480	06/08/2015
	WYW	184487	06/10/2015
	WYW	184488	06/10/2015
	WYW	184510	07/06/2015
	WYW	184525	07/22/2015
	WYW	184576	08/03/2015

Rawlins Field Office Total	31		
Rock Springs Field Office	WYW	163790	09/02/2005
	WYW	167539	10/01/2007
	WYW	167631	07/24/2008
	WYW	167799	06/03/2011
	WYW	167841	11/18/2011
	WYW	167857	04/12/2012
	WYW	167859	04/27/2012
	WYW	167867	06/11/2012
	WYW	167873	07/18/2012
	WYW	167874	07/18/2012
	WYW	167887	10/02/2012
	WYW	167899	11/15/2012
	WYW	167908	02/28/2013
	WYW	167909	03/13/2013
	WYW	167915	03/15/2013
	WYW	167918	04/11/2013
	WYW	167919	04/11/2013
	WYW	183364	04/03/2014
	WYW	183687	06/03/2014
	WYW	184470	06/08/2015
	WYW	184482	06/22/2015
	WYW	184500	06/26/2015
	WYW	184499	07/06/2015
	WYW	184527	07/23/2015
	WYW	184529	07/24/2015
	WYW	184530	07/24/2015
Rock Springs Field Office Total	31		
Worland Field Office	WYW	162898	08/02/2005
	WYW	165321	05/29/2014
Worland Field Office Total	2		
WY TOTAL	111		
BLM TOTAL	867		

Question 5: Secretary Jewell has stated that BLM will propose a new rule for flaring and venting of natural gas on federal lands and Indian lands shortly.

Does BLM plan to conduct a federalism assessment on the impacts of the proposed rule to states pursuant to Executive Order 13132? If not, why not?

Response:

Executive Order 13132 requires preparation of a federalism assessment if a rule would have a substantial direct effect on the states, or the relationship between the national government and the states, or on the distribution of power and responsibilities among the levels of government. At this time, the BLM has not yet issued a proposed rule for flaring and venting of natural gas from leases administered by the BLM, including leases on public lands and Indian lands. Thus, we have not yet made a final determination regarding whether preparation of a federalism assessment would be required for this rule.

Questions from Senator Lisa Murkowski

Question 1: **The Montana BLM office already oversees the North Dakota mineral activities, and Washington state and Oregon activities are managed out of the Portland office. E&E reported March 13, 2015 that there is speculation of a merger of the New Mexico and Arizona BLM offices. Is consolidation of the state offices part of a larger policy vision for the future organizational structure of the BLM, and if so, what impacts and results does the BLM anticipate from such a shift?**

Response:

The BLM remains committed to directing our budget to areas where we can make the greatest positive impact for the nation.

Declining budgets and sequestration have eroded the BLM's ability to deliver the services and programs that the public expects from us. Because of increasing pressure on the BLM's budget, the agency's staffing level has dropped by 1,300 positions or 12 percent over the past five years. Not only has the BLM's budget declined in real dollar terms, but fixed costs have also increased substantially, further reducing the BLM's purchasing power. This serious decline in agency resources and personnel has come at the same time that public interest in and public use of our nation's public lands is increasing. As a result, the BLM must always be looking for ways to use our budget and personnel more efficiently.

As part of our responsibility to align our remaining budget and personnel resources to maximize our efforts, the BLM is always looking at potential efficiencies, which can include structural realignments. The BLM explored the possibility of combining its Arizona and New Mexico state offices to better serve the public in the southwest by directing more resources to the district and field office level. After listening carefully to feedback from partners and stakeholders, the BLM has decided not to move forward with a merger of these two state offices.

Question 2: **You stated during the hearing that significant consultations with States and Tribes occurred in the development of the rule. Did BLM consult with the State of Alaska, the Alaska Oil and Gas Conservation Commission, Alaska Native Village or Regional Corporations or tribal councils? Please list the entities in Alaska with whom the BLM consulted in the development of this rule.**

Response:

During the four years spent developing the hydraulic fracturing rule, the BLM consulted with many states with significant oil and gas operations and benefited from their experience and expertise. In Alaska, the BLM consulted with the Alaska Oil and Gas Conservation Commission and Alaska Department of Environmental Conservation. In addition, during the rulemaking process, the BLM paid particular attention to the State of

Alaska's regulations addressing interwell communications, or "frack hits." (20 AAC 25.283, *Hydraulic Fracturing,* published in August 2014)

Tribal consultation was a similarly critical component of this rulemaking effort, and the Department remains committed to making sure tribal leaders play a significant role as the BLM and tribes work together to develop resources on public and Indian lands in a safe and responsible way. For the rulemaking effort, the BLM initiated government-to-government consultation with tribes on the proposed rule and offered to hold follow-up consultation meetings with any tribe that desired to have an individual meeting. Many subsequent meetings were held with individual tribes. In January 2012, the BLM held four regional tribal consultation meetings, to which over 175 tribal entities were invited. These group meetings were followed by individual consultation meetings, with the latter involving local BLM authorized officers and management, including State Directors in recognition of established local relationships.

In June 2012, the BLM held additional regional consultation meetings in Salt Lake City, Utah; Farmington, New Mexico; Tulsa, Oklahoma; and Billings, Montana. Eighty-one tribal members representing 27 tribes attended the meetings. In these sessions, the BLM and tribal representatives engaged in substantive discussions of the proposed hydraulic fracturing rule. A variety of issues were discussed, including but not limited to the applicability of tribal laws, validating water sources, inspection and enforcement, wellbore integrity, and water management, among others. Additional individual consultations with tribal representatives have taken place since that time. Consultation meetings were also held at the National Congress of American Indian Conference in Lincoln, Nebraska, on June 18, 2012, and at New Town, North Dakota on July 13, 2012. Although the BLM did not have a specific tribal consultation session in the State of Alaska, the BLM undertook a robust tribal consultation process for the rule.

Questions from Senator Jeff Flake

Question 1: On Friday, April 24, BLM Deputy Director Steve Ellis held a congressional briefing on a proposal to merge the Arizona and New Mexico state BLM offices. Can you provide an update on the status of that decision making process? That is, when does BLM plan to make a decision?

Response:

After listening carefully to feedback from partners and stakeholders, the BLM has decided not to move forward with a merger of these two State Offices. The BLM is maintaining both the Arizona and New Mexico State Offices and both State Director positions.

Question 2: If BLM decides to move forward with merging the offices, what sort of notice and consultation is the Bureau required to engage in with Congress before finalizing its decision?

Response:

After listening carefully to feedback from partners and stakeholders, the BLM has decided not to move forward with a merger of these two State Offices. The BLM is maintaining both the Arizona and New Mexico State Offices and both State Director positions.

Question 3: What type of outreach has the BLM conducted with interested stakeholders in Arizona and New Mexico?

Response:

After listening carefully to feedback from partners and stakeholders, the BLM has decided not to move forward with a merger of these two State Offices. The BLM is maintaining both the Arizona and New Mexico State Offices and both State Director positions..

Question 4: During the briefing, Deputy Secretary Ellis made frequent references to the joint offices in Oregon and Washington, as well as Montana and the Dakotas. Please provide information on the average length of time it takes those offices to process permits, environmental analyses, and other approvals before and after those officer mergers were completed.

Response:

BLM Deputy Director, Operations, Steve Ellis made references to Montana and the Dakotas and Oregon and Washington offices to illustrate that the BLM has experience of effectively managing across state boundaries. These multi-state organizations have been in place in one form or another since the early days of the BLM, before the passage of the National Environmental Policy Act of 1969 or the Federal Land Policy and Management Act of 1976. Because of this, before and after processing times are unavailable.

Question 5: Please provide information on the cost savings that were realized from prior BLM office mergers (e.g., Oregon-Washington, Montana-Dakotas), and whether those cost savings were retained by those new regional offices or used elsewhere in the Bureau.

Response:

These multi-state organizations have been in place in one form or another since the early days of the BLM, before the passage of the National Environmental Policy Act of 1969 or the Federal Land Policy and Management Act of 1976. Because of this, before and after costs are unavailable.

Questions from Senator Mazie K. Hirono

Question 1: BLM MOU with FracFocus

At the time that the Bureau of Land Management published the final rule on hydraulic fracturing on public lands the agency indicated that it was entering into a MOU with the managers of FracFocus to clear up concerns and recommendations by the Department of Energy's Science Advisory Board relating to functionality and accessibility of data.

Can you explain in more detail the specifics of the MOU? Does it address all recommendations and actions in the Department of Energy's FracFocus 2.0 report or only a portion of those?

Response:

The BLM is working closely with the Ground Water Protection Council (GWPC) to finalize a Memorandum of Understanding (MOU) that will ensure that industry's disclosures of chemicals used in the hydraulic fracturing process can be easily searched and downloaded from the GWPC's publicly available database, FracFocus. The BLM is also collaborating with the Department of Energy (DOE) and will address the DOE's FracFocus report recommendations in the MOU.

Question 2: Environmental Impacts of Fracking

The New Yorker **recently ran a lengthy piece that discussed the linkage between oil and gas development and the frequency of earthquake activity in Oklahoma. It noted that "Until 2008, Oklahoma experienced an average of one to two earthquakes of 3.0 magnitude or greater each year. In 2014, there were five hundred and eighty-five, nearly triple the rate of California. Including smaller earthquakes in the count, there were more than five thousand."**

The article goes on to say, "Disposal wells trigger earthquakes when they are dug too deep, near or into basement rock, or when the wells impinge on a fault line." The research geologist from the United States Geological Survey that was interviewed for the article said, when discussing the linkage, "Scientifically, it's really quite clear." Do you agree with the USGS geologist that oil and gas exploration has contributed to increased seismic activity? Do you believe that additional steps should be taken to limit hydraulic fracturing or better regulate the placement of disposal wells, which house wastewater from hydraulic fracturing, in areas known to trigger earthquakes?

Response:

The USGS report[i] you referenced summarized the issue of induced seismicity as follows:

> Although enhanced oil recovery and hydraulic fracturing have been implicated in some recent seismicity, studies indicate that the majority of the increase in

seismicity is induced by the deep disposal of fluids produced by oil and gas production (wastewater disposal). Hydraulic fracturing does not play a key role in the increase in that 1) hydraulic fracturing does not typically induce felt earthquakes; 2) in Oklahoma, the location of the largest increase in seismicity, spent hydraulic fracturing fluid does not represent a large percentage of the fluids comprising disposed wastewater; and 3) oil produced from many fields with large volumes of produced water did not involve any hydraulic fracturing.

Disposal wells are principally regulated by the U.S. Environmental Protection Agency and the states or tribes. A proposal to locate a disposal well on surface managed by BLM requires BLM's approval. The USGS report does suggest that attention to the siting of disposal wells is prudent.

---

[i] Myths and Facts on Wastewater Injection, Hydraulic Fracturing, Enhanced Oil Recovery, and Induced Seismicity, Justin L. Rubinstein and Alireza Babaie Mahani, Seismological Research Letters Volume 86, Number 4 July/August 2015, https://profile.usgs.gov/myscience/upload_folder/ci2015Jun1012005755600Induced_EQs_Review.pdf

EARTHWORKS

U.S. Senate Committee on Energy and Natural Resources Subcommittee on Public Lands, Forests, and Mining
April 30, 2015 Hearing: The BLM's Final Rule on Hydraulic Fracturing

Answers in Response to Questions for the Record Submitted to Mr. Bruce Baizel

Answers for the Honorable Senator Mazie K. Hirono

Question 1: Timing and Transparency of Chemical Disclosure

Thank you Senator Hirono for this question. You are correct that the proposed Bureau of Land Management (BLM) rule on hydraulic fracturing only requires chemical disclosure within 30 days following injection. As you note, some states like Wyoming, already require pre-fracturing disclosure. That a major oil and gas producing state like Wyoming can compel operators to disclose their frack fluids before injection shows that industry objections to the feasibility of pre-fracturing disclosure have no merit.

For the purposes of protecting communities and dwindling usable water supplies in Western states, only pre-drilling disclosure will adequately protect landowners and public safety. First, landowners need to know what chemicals to test for, if they intend to get their water wells tested, pre-drilling, as a protection against contamination by the oil or gas company's activities. Therefore, they need a complete list of all chemicals to be used in drilling or fracturing before those operations take place.

Second, in many cases where problems emerge, the structural integrity of the well fails during drilling or completion, including fracturing, due to the high pressures and volumes injected. Under these regulations, those chemicals would ordinarily remain secret at the time of the well failure. Emergency responders, medical professionals, and the public need to know the chemicals because, in the event of an emergency, disclosure after the fact comes too late.

A specific, and almost tragic, example of this problem comes from my community of Durango, Colorado in 2008. Cathy Behr worked as an emergency room nurse at Mercy Regional Medical Center in Durango[i]. When a patient entered the emergency room after getting caught in a fracturing fluid spill, Ms. Behr treated him. But a few days later, Ms. Behr was admitted to the ICU with a swollen liver and fluid in her lungs. Doctors diagnosed her with chemical poisoning; however, they were unable to identify the chemicals in the fracking fluid, and ultimately ended up making an educated 'guess' as to the treatment that Ms. Behr required.

If regulators require operators to disclose all chemical ingredients in fracturing fluid before drilling, emergency responders would have a better chance of diagnosing symptoms while protecting themselves and others.

Question 2: Environmental Impacts of Fracking

Thank you Senator Hirono for this question. Yes. The scientific consensus is increasingly clear: that injection of fracking wastewater can and sometimes does induce seismic activity. In addition to the United States Geological Survey, researchers from Southern Methodist University in Texas have reached similar conclusions[ii]. The Oklahoma Geological Survey has also recently clarified its view that injection of waste associated with oil and gas production is the likely primary cause of increased seismicity in Oklahoma.[iii] Much more study is needed in this area[iv].

In the interim, regulators should place an immediate moratorium on wastewater injection in those areas known to be subject to earthquakes until additional steps can be implemented to help ensure public health and safety.

Initial steps that operators and regulators can take to mitigate the risk of earthquakes include: limiting wastewater volumes and pressures, siting disposal wells farther away from both surface structures and all underground fault lines, and additional seismicity testing and monitoring. This committee can find useful guidance in the regulations found under the Safe Drinking Water Act's Underground Injection Control (UIC) program for Class I wells, where a number of these precautions are already required. Most importantly, municipalities that have experienced earthquakes resulting from fracking wastewater injection need to have clear authority to regulate the location of these wells under their zoning powers so as to best protect their communities.

Thank you, once again, for the opportunity to address your questions. If I can be of any further help to you or to the Committee, please do not hesitate to ask.

---

[i] Oil & Gas Exploration: Is "Fracking" Safe? By Jim Moscou *Newsweek* 8/19/08 http://www.newsweek.com/oil-gas-exploration-fracking-safe-87557
[ii] SMU-UT Study Shows "Plausible" Connection Between DFW Quakes and Saltwater Injection Well
[iii] Please see http://wichita.ogs.ou.edu/documents/OGS_Statement-Earthquakes-4-21-15.pdf
[iv] Earthworks has authored a study *Shaky Ground: How Oil Companies Increase California's Earthquake Risk*.
More information can be found on our Fracking-related Earthquakes issue page.

U.S. Senate Committee on Energy and Natural Resources
Subcommittee on Public Lands, Forests, and Mining
April 30, 2015 Hearing: The BLM's Final Rule on Hydraulic Fracturing
Questions for the Record Submitted to Ms. Kathleen Sgamma

Questions from Senator Lisa Murkowski

Question 1: A 2009 Ground Water Protection Council study concluded "(t)he regulation of oil and gas field activities is managed best at the state level where regional and local conditions are understood and where regulations can be tailored to fit the needs of the local environment."[1] Part of this assessment was premised on the states' ability to readily perform field inspections, enforcement and oversight in addition to be onsite for well operations, testing and plugging. In your experience, does and will the BLM have sufficient bandwidth, expertise, and resources to similarly conduct on the ground inspections, oversight, et cetera?

Answer 1: Western Energy Alliance agrees with GWPC that regulation is best done by the states. BLM does not have the capability to meet its current obligations, much less implement a new hydraulic fracturing rule. Onshore leasing is down 54% since 2008; only three major oil and natural gas projects have been approved during the Obama Administration while BLM continues to delay project approval under the National Environmental Policy Act (NEPA); and permitting takes an average of 227 days.[2]

Support for GWPC's conclusion comes from an unlikely source, the Western Organization of Resource Councils (WORC), an environmental group. WORC publishes I&E data periodically to make the point that there should be more inspections of oil and natural gas activity.[3] While WORC's conclusion is the typical conclusion of the environmental lobby, i.e., federal regulation is always needed, the actual data in the report tells a different story. Taking the data in the report and doing a simple ratio of the number of inspections compared to the number of active wells shows that states are indeed more effective than the federal government when it comes to I&E. BLM had the lowest rate of inspections compared to the states analyzed in the report, at 21%.

If the goal is public health, safety and environmental protection, then the states are the correct place to regulate. If the goal is centralized, federal control and not real environmental protection, then additional federal regulation is the answer. Western Energy Alliance believes true environmental protection is better done at the state level, and that is why we are legally challenging the new BLM fracking rule.

---

[1] *State Oil and Natural Gas Regulations Designed to Protect Water Resources*, pg. 6.
[2] BLM NEPA approvals of three years or more are preventing development from projects that could generate 101,000 jobs and $25 billion in annual economic impact. See our NEPA delays study, conducted by SWCA Environmental Consultants.
[3] *Law and Order in the Oil and Gas Fields: A Review of the Inspection and Enforcement Programs in Five Western States*, WORC, 2013.

U.S. Senate Committee on Energy and Natural Resources
Subcommittee on Public Lands, Forests, and Mining
April 30, 2015 Hearing: The BLM's Final Rule on Hydraulic Fracturing
Questions for the Record Submitted to Ms. Kathleen Sgamma

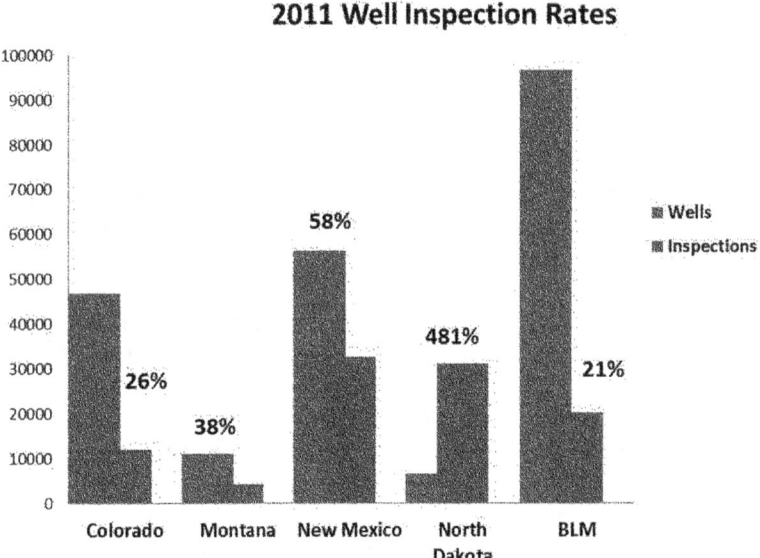

Source: Graph from Western Energy Alliance using data provided by WORC

Western Energy Alliance has heard from several staff in the western BLM state and field offices who have indicated that they do not have the resources to implement the new fracking rule. The decision to move forward with a rule that is redundant with state regulation was ill-advised, given the lack of resources allocated to the BLM field offices and the lack of wherewithal to implement an entirely new regulatory regime. BLM and Interior Secretary Jewell often complain that the agency does not have sufficient resources for inspection and enforcement (I&E), yet it is a matter of how BLM chooses to use its resources. Certainly BLM could use its resources to effectively manage the onshore oil and natural gas program and conduct more I&E and other oversight, but has chosen instead to divert resources to renewable energy, restructure the planning process in ways contrary to Federal Land Policy and Management Act and basic federalism principles, add new layers of NEPA analysis and new regulations, and otherwise self-impose a myriad of other requirements that take staff out of the field and put them behind desks pushing paper. BLM has chosen to use its bandwidth on other priorities than oil and natural gas I&E.

Question 2: The Montana BLM office already oversees the North Dakota mineral activities. E&E reported March 13, 2015 that there is speculation of a merger of the New Mexico and Arizona BLM offices. Given your testimony on the 'inability to implement' the new hydraulic fracking rule, in your opinion, what effect would such a merger have on the BLM's ability to manage federal mineral resources in the southwest?

U.S. Senate Committee on Energy and Natural Resources
Subcommittee on Public Lands, Forests, and Mining
April 30, 2015 Hearing: The BLM's Final Rule on Hydraulic Fracturing
Questions for the Record Submitted to Ms. Kathleen Sgamma

<u>Answer 2:</u> Western Energy Alliance is concerned about efforts to combine the New Mexico and Arizona BLM state offices under one regional director. We are concerned the consolidation would result in less efficient land management without providing any of the intended long-term cost savings.

BLM has traditionally operated on a state-by-state basis, which allows each office to have intimate knowledge of the issues faced in each individual state. In contrast to this model, the proposed consolidation would establish a state office with responsibility for managing BLM lands and resources in five states.

As it stands, the New Mexico BLM office is currently responsible for four states – New Mexico, Oklahoma, Texas, and Kansas. This regional approach is unique in the western United States, but it is practical because the federal land and mineral acreage in Oklahoma, Texas, and Kansas totals only 7.4 million acres. By contrast, BLM in Arizona administers 12.2 million surface acres and another 17.5 million subsurface acres within the state. The addition of Arizona and its large federal acreage to the New Mexico office would only serve to further divide resources in a manner that is not compatible with BLM's mission, and would limit the time and attention the State Director and associated staff may reasonably be expected to devote to oil and natural gas development and production.

Furthermore, New Mexico and Arizona present significantly different management challenges for BLM. The expertise that is required of the director in each state is substantially different. Combining the New Mexico and Arizona State Offices into one entity would lead to gaps in the knowledge necessary to effectively manage the diverse lands and resources that would fall under the purview of the new position. For instance, mining issues and national park management are crucial in Arizona, whereas the New Mexico office oversees significant oil and natural gas resources with less exposure to national park management.

Finally, we are concerned this proposal has not undergone the proper evaluation necessary for such an impactful decision. We are aware that, in a time of constrained budgets, consolidation is often discussed as a cost-cutting measure. However, no analysis of the possible budgetary effects of this proposal has been released at this time, and the savings typically associated with these actions are generally over-promised and under-delivered. Oil and natural gas development in New Mexico is a significant revenue generator for the federal and state governments. According to the Office of Natural Resource Revenue, oil and natural gas federal tax and royalty payments totaled more than $1 billion in 2013. Lack of attention and a dilution of resources away from the oil and natural gas program could actually result in less revenue and substantially overshadow any administrative costs savings from an office consolidation.

U.S. Senate Committee on Energy and Natural Resources
Subcommittee on Public Lands, Forests, and Mining
April 30, 2015 Hearing: The BLM's Final Rule on Hydraulic Fracturing
Questions for the Record Submitted to Ms. Kathleen Sgamma

Questions from Senator Mazie K. Hirono

<u>**Question 1:**</u> **Impacts of Fracking on Water Supply**
The U.S. Drought Monitor indicated that as of April 21st all 11 states considered in the western region had at least one county affected by drought-impacting over 53 million people and we haven't even gotten to summer here in the Northern Hemisphere. I know that fracking is a very water-intensive industry that has potential to greatly impact water resources in western communities.

Can you discuss measures that your members are taking to address the decreasing water supply out west? In deciding where companies will frack, are considerations taken regarding the hydrologic impacts to the surrounding communities? Is the industry taking measures to increase water use efficiency?

<u>Answer 1:</u> The good news is that even though fracking use a tiny portion of states' water, companies are continually decreasing fresh water use by developing new technologies, reusing ancient waters produced from miles deep underground that would otherwise not be brought to the earth's surface, and treating and recycling water. By continuing to innovate, industry continues to use less water. The Energy Water Initiative group of producers has documented several water management case studies that I recommend for particular examples of how the industry is reducing water use.[4]

Golder Associates, an environmental consultancy, conducted an analysis of water use in the West for Western Energy Alliance. Each state tracks water use a bit differently, but total oil and natural gas development and production, not just hydraulic fracturing, uses a very small percent in each major production state of the Rocky Mountain West. For example in Colorado, total industrial water use accounts for 0.8% of the state's total water. Since oil and natural gas is just a subset of that industrial category, total use is much lower than 0.8%, although the exact number is not possible to discern from the available data. However, according to the Deputy State Engineer, the amount of water used for hydraulic fracturing in 2012 was less than 14,000 acre-ft, or 0.07% of all water used statewide. New Mexico provides another example from a major producing state, where total oil and natural gas use, including fracking, represents 0.06% of total water use.

Nationwide, oil and natural gas represents about 0.025% of total daily water use[5] while providing 62% of total energy. That represents a good balance of water use while providing the energy that powers the economy and the feedstock for an abundance of consumer good, from cosmetics and pharmaceuticals to clothing and sports equipment.

---

[4] *U.S. Onshore Unconventional Exploration and Production Water Management Case Studies,* CH2MHill prepared for the Energy Water Initiative, January 2015.
[5] *Total Water Use in the United States, 2005,* U.S. Geological Service.

U.S. Senate Committee on Energy and Natural Resources
Subcommittee on Public Lands, Forests, and Mining
April 30, 2015 Hearing: The BLM's Final Rule on Hydraulic Fracturing
Questions for the Record Submitted to Ms. Kathleen Sgamma

Compared to other energy sources, unconventional oil and natural gas development which is made possible by fracking, is one of the least water-intensive fuel sources.[6]

Despite that small water use, oil and natural gas companies continue to become more efficient and reduce water use, both on principle because it's the right thing to do and for economic reasons. Because companies usually do not own water rights, they must purchase fresh water locally. Therefore, there's a built in incentive to reduce water use. Since water is purchased on the market, there is a self-correcting mechanism to address any local water constraints; as water becomes scarce, the price increases, and companies further reduce water use.

Returning to the subject of the hearing, the new BLM hydraulic fracturing rule, not only does it not contain provisions to reduce water use, its unintended consequences could be to make it more difficult to treat and reuse water on public lands. Rigid requirements on tank size and prohibition of pits will hamper innovative centralized fluids gathering and processing facilities. Centralized facilities not only minimize surface disturbance, but also enable water treatment on a large enough scale to maximize water reuse and recycling. As a result of the rigid requirements, water management processing will be more difficult on public lands, even as water reuse and recycling are increased on private and state lands.

Question 2: Environmental Impacts of Fracking
The New Yorker recently ran a lengthy piece that discussed the linkage between oil and gas development and the frequency of earthquake activity in Oklahoma. It noted that "Until 2008, Oklahoma experienced an average of one to two earthquakes of 3.0 magnitude or greater each year. In 2014, there were five hundred and eighty-five, nearly triple the rate of California. Including smaller earthquakes in the count, there were more than five thousand."

The article goes on to say, "Disposal wells trigger earthquakes when they are dug too deep, near or into basement rock, or when the wells impinge on a fault line." The research geologist from the United States Geological Survey that was interviewed for the article said, when discussing the linkage, "Scientifically, it's really quite clear." Do you agree with the USGS geologist that oil and gas exploration has contributed to increased seismic activity? Do you believe that additional steps should be taken to limit hydraulic fracturing or better regulate the placement of disposal wells, which house wastewater from hydraulic fracturing, in areas known to trigger earthquakes?

Answer 2: Again, the BLM hydraulic fracturing rule does nothing to address seismic activity from oil and natural gas development. The issue of induced seismic activity associated with oil and natural gas development arises from the disposal of produced and

---

[6] *Water Consumption of Energy Resource Extraction, Processing and Conversion*, Erik Mielke et al., Harvard Kennedy School, Belfer Center for Science and International Affairs, October 2010.

U.S. Senate Committee on Energy and Natural Resources
Subcommittee on Public Lands, Forests, and Mining
April 30, 2015 Hearing: The BLM's Final Rule on Hydraulic Fracturing
Questions for the Record Submitted to Ms. Kathleen Sgamma

other waste waters, not from fracking itself. It is clear from USGS and other studies that there has been increased seismic activity from a small number of disposal wells that are used to store fluids from oil and natural gas development. The answer is not to limit hydraulic fracturing, but to ensure disposal wells are sited in appropriate, stable geological formations and that the pressure and volumes of wastewater are suitable for that geology. States are already regulating disposal wells and responding to new information on seismicity.

Underground injection control (UIC) disposal wells are regulated as Class II wells in accordance with the Safe Drinking Water Act through delegation of primacy from EPA to the states. The states have been very responsive to the incidents of earthquakes felt at the surface and have tightened regulations to reduce the risk. Most of the seismic activity experienced from UIC wells are not felt at the surface. Where incidents have occurred, states have taken action to strengthen their UIC requirements to ensure disposal wells are situated in stable geology and at the appropriate pressure and volume so that earthquakes are not triggered.

As USGS has pointed out, "Of more than 150,000 Class II injection wells in the United States, roughly 40,000 are waste fluid disposal wells for oil and gas operations. **Only a small fraction** of these disposal wells have induced earthquakes that are large enough to be of concern to the public."[7] (emphasis added)

---

[7] http://www.usgs.gov/faq/categories/9833/3424

U.S. Senate Committee on Energy and Natural Resources
Subcommittee on Public Lands, Forests, and Mining
April 30, 2015 Hearing: The BLM's Final Rule on Hydraulic Fracturing
Questions for the Record Submitted to Mr. Mark Watson

Questions from Senator Mazie K. Hirono

Question 1: Impacts of Fracking on Water Supply

The U.S. Drought Monitor indicated that as of April 21st all 11 states considered in the western region had at least one county affected by drought-impacting over 53 million people and we haven't even gotten to summer here in the Northern Hemisphere. I know that fracking is a very water-intensive industry that has potential to greatly impact water resources in western communities.

Can you discuss measures that your members are taking to address the decreasing water supply out west? In deciding where companies will frack, are considerations taken regarding the hydrologic impacts to the surrounding communities? Is the industry taking measures to increase water use efficiency?

Question 2: Environmental Impacts of Fracking

The New Yorker recently ran a lengthy piece that discussed the linkage between oil and gas development and the frequency of earthquake activity in Oklahoma. It noted that "Until 2008, Oklahoma experienced an average of one to two earthquakes of 3.0 magnitude or greater each year. In 2014, there were five hundred and eighty-five, nearly triple the rate of California. Including smaller earthquakes in the count, there were more than five thousand."

The article goes on to say, "Disposal wells trigger earthquakes when they are dug too deep, near or into basement rock, or when the wells impinge on a fault line." The research geologist from the United States Geological Survey that was interviewed for the article said, when discussing the linkage, "Scientifically, it's really quite clear." Do you agree with the USGS geologist that oil and gas exploration has contributed to increased seismic activity? Do you believe that additional steps should be taken to limit hydraulic fracturing or better regulate the placement of disposal wells, which house wastewater from hydraulic fracturing, in areas known to trigger earthquakes?

U.S Senate Committee on Energy and Natural Resources

Subcommittee on Public Lands, Forests, and Mining

April 30, 2015 Hearing: The BLM's Final Rule on Hydraulic Fracturing

Questions for the Record Submitted to Mr. Mark Watson

Questions from Senator Mazie K. Hirono

Question 1: Impacts of Fracking on Water Supply

Wyoming has abundant sources of water that is used in the fracking process, unlike some other states. However, the energy industry has been very proactive in reducing water usage and several operators in Wyoming are re-cycling produced water for use in hydraulic fracturing. In fact, a recent article in the Wall Street Journal showed examples of water saving efforts including a waste water treatment plant used by an operator and built by GE.

Question 2: Environmental Impacts of Fracking, specifically induced seismicity

As a petroleum engineer, I do not have the technical expertise to answer the specific question. However, I have reviewed a recent report on this subject and it appears that it is plausible that injection wells, permitting under EPA's UIC Program, may have a direct correlation to seismic activities in States such as Oklahoma and Ohio. The Wyoming State Geologic Survey recently published a report showing that no seismic activity in Wyoming can be attributed to injections wells or hydraulically fractured wells.